ENDORSEMENTS

"*This book is a rare blend of depth, clarity, and soul. Susanne has coached some of the most successful C-suite leaders and now, through these pages, offers that same powerful insight to the rest of us. It's not a book you just read; it's a book you experience. If you're ready to lead with authenticity, courage, and impact, this is your only guide.*"

—Declan Grant, President at Aeromed Group

"*The book every leader wishes they had at the start, and the one they need now—because true leadership begins with mastering the voice within.*"

—John Rose, former President, Nuheat Industries Ltd.

"*Susanne brings the same rare combination of insight, discipline, and compassion to this book that she brings to her coaching. It's a generous, deeply human guide to becoming more self-aware and effective, offering proof that her remarkable gift for transformation extends well beyond the coaching space.*"

—Graeme Keirstead, K.C. Deputy Registrar/ Chief Legal Counsel, College of Physicians and Surgeons of BC

"*I have been fortunate to work with Susanne one-on-one, and she takes abstract leadership principles and makes them deeply personal, implementable, and powerful. This Could Be Everything is for anyone who wants to lead—not just with their title, but with their whole self. Read this book and prepare to change the way you think about leadership forever.*"

—Michael Van Aken, Chief Human Resources Officer, Acosta

i

"The difference that makes the difference in both leadership and life lies in what we do on the inside. A book every executive needs on their desk."

—Nancy MacKay, Founder & CEO, MacKay CEO Forums

"Susanne has beautifully captured her incredible gift to see people who have entrusted her to witness their journey on becoming the best version of themselves. This work is real, necessary and some of the most rewarding work one can do to live a fulfilling, energizing and exceptional life."

—Angela Santiago, CEO and Co-Founder,
The Little Potato Company

"This is the book I wish I had 15 years ago. Susanne has been a guiding force in my life; wise, intuitive, and profoundly human. She brings life, light, and color to leadership, transforming it from something we do into who we are. This isn't just a leadership book; it's a revolution in how we see and show up as leaders."

—Fiona Macintyre. Founder, Forming Impact

"I've had the privilege of working directly with Susanne and this book beautifully reflects what's at the heart of her transformative coaching style. After years of wanting and waiting for the next thing, in executive leadership and in life, Susanne taught me to embrace the true me. Making the connection between being authentically myself and leading joyfully has given me a freedom I could never have imagined. I show up better for everyone in my life. This Could Be Everything is an invitation to lead with your whole self—not just your position. Let this book open your eyes and your heart, and you'll never see leadership the same way again."

—Heather Brennan, Ph.D., President, Lumisque Inc.

"Susanne Biro has written a powerful guide for anyone ready to step into deeper leadership and a fuller life. This Could Be Everything is equal parts wisdom, clarity, and courage."

—Asanka Pathiraja, Emerging Growth Investor,
Manhattan Lawyer, Wildlife Photographer

"I've known Susanne for almost a decade, and her wisdom has continually challenged and inspired me. Reading This Could Be Everything feels like sitting across from her...clear-eyed, compassionate, and challenging in the best way. She shows us that the inner work we often avoid is exactly what shapes not only our leadership but our entire life. This book is an invitation to freedom, presence, and real impact."

—Ginger Jones, Serial Entrepreneur, Founder,
Next Mile Network

"In a time of accelerating change, increasing complexity and a great deal of uncertainty, we need to rethink effective leadership. In her book Susanne provides practical, thought-provoking insights you can apply immediately and with great impact. It's exactly what is needed right now."

—Marion Burchell, Managing Director, Azolla & Adjunct
Faculty at AGSM

"Susanne Biro has created something remarkable—a book that transcends its corporate leadership framework to speak to anyone seeking meaningful transformation. I found myself highlighting passages, completing exercises, and immediately incorporating her wisdom into my own work. Susanne's guidance on making tomorrow better than today isn't just theory—it's a practical roadmap I've already begun using in my daily, weekly, and annual

practices. While we share some similar philosophies, Susanne speaks with her own distinctive voice and depth born from decades of coaching experience. This Could Be Everything delivers exactly what its title promises: everything you need to step into your full potential, regardless of where you are in your journey."

—Terri Hanson Mead, author, Piloting Your Life

"Leadership isn't about tactics—it's about becoming who you truly are with more skill. This Could Be Everything is a beautiful challenge for you to examine your habits, beliefs, and impact on others. And although the focus is on leadership, this is also a series of conversations about your whole life, living with wisdom, integrity and purpose. It's authenticated by what I've seen Susanne live first-hand through her coaching practice and her own life over the years. Highly recommended."

—Russell McCann, Formula 1 Performance Coach

"In today's world of relentless complexity and pressure for results, Susanne reminds us that the true essence of leadership is not found in strategy or metrics, but in self-awareness. I've taken time to let this book percolate, with moments of deep resonance and others that made me pause and take stock. It is a beautiful, transformative guide to becoming the kind of leader the world truly needs. Bravo!"

—Terry VanQuickenborne, Coach and Leadership Strategist; Former Vice President of Research, The Josh Bersin Company, and Global Head of Learning & Organization Development, Autodesk.

THIS COULD BE EVERYTHING

For Anyone Who Wants to Make
Their Tomorrow Better Than Today

SUSANNE BIRO

This Could Be Everything: For Anyone Who Wants to Make Their Tomorrow Better Than Today

Written by Susanne Biro

Copyright © 2025 Susanne Biro
Cover designed by Wesley Bryant

This book is a work of nonfiction. It represents the accuracy of the events mentioned to the best of the author's recollection. Some names in the book have been replaced to maintain the privacy of certain individuals.

Hardcover ISBN: 978-1-0699210-2-4
Paperback ISBN: 978-1-0699210-1-7
eBook ISBN: 978-0699210-0-0

The information contained in this book is provided for educational purposes only and should not be construed as legal or financial advice. Readers are strongly encouraged to consult with a qualified and licensed professional who can provide advice tailored to their individual circumstances. Laws, regulations, and financial practices vary across countries, states, and regions. Market conditions, returns, and outcomes will differ over time and cannot be guaranteed. While every effort has been made to provide accurate and timely information at the time of writing, we make no representations or warranties regarding completeness, accuracy, or applicability. We are not making any official legal or financial recommendations. The examples, figures, and principles presented herein are for illustrative and educational purposes only. Any decisions you make are solely your responsibility.

DEDICATION

To those I love most, who fill my life with meaning—

To Elfie and Geza Biro, the most incredible parents,
thank you for loving me, keeping me safe,
and telling me I could do anything
I set my mind to. I miss you both terribly.

To Chris, I love you and the life we have built.
Let's keep dreaming together!

To Ben and Georgia, you are our world. Always remember you
can do anything you set your mind to and that you are loved
endlessly and forever. Being your mom is the greatest joy of
my life. May you shine brightly and light the world with your
vision, your values, and your dreams.

To Sharon and Karin, thank you for your wise mentorship and
guidance throughout my entire life. You are everything to me.

To Stacey, the most gifted leadership development practitioner
I know and the truest friend one could wish for. You live all
we seek to teach. Thank you for your endless support and
encouragement as I wrote this book.

And finally, to all the clients I have had the honor of working
with, thank you for trusting me. Every single one of you
inspired me with your humanity, your humility,
and your desire to become better.

BOOK BONUS

Excited to dive in? You should be.

This book holds the key to what truly matters: your health, happiness, and success in leadership and life. The insights and tools within these pages have the power to transform your entire experience of life—**if you apply them.**

To help you do just that, I've created a special bonus: **a curated collection of podcast recordings** that will bring these ideas to life in ways that are practical, actionable, and inspiring.

Claim your exclusive **BOOK BONUS** at: **SusanneBiro.com/Book-Bonus**

TABLE OF CONTENTS

CHAPTER ONE

WELCOME!

What if I told you there was a way of thinking that would not only improve your leadership and impact but potentially transform every single moment you ever experience? Would you be interested?

The thoughts you entertain each day shape your perception and become your reality. But what you call reality is only one interpretation; there are others. By choosing the thoughts you allow into your mind, you have the power to profoundly improve your life.

And to truly benefit others, your organization, your family, your community, and the world, you must first be well within yourself, as we can never truly lead, love, or lift others until we've learned how to lead, love, and lift ourselves. But to do so, we must face our own humanity: our fears and insecurities and the pain that power and success can't fix.

In this book, I'll guide you through the real frontier of leadership: your mind, because your inner thoughts and feelings always determine your performance "out there."

My goal is to facilitate one clear outcome: that you become your self—the best, highest, most you *you*, and in doing so, you allow yourself to experience the freedom, fulfillment, impact, and real success you seek.

Today…and every day.

After all, who wants to wait to start fully enjoying their life?

The following chapters are structured as lessons drawn from my background in psychology, business, communications, leadership, executive coaching, and applied behavioral science.

More importantly, they are derived from my firsthand experience working closely with thousands of senior-level leaders. Some have led global teams across multiple continents. Others have reached the pinnacle of corporate or founder success.

Just know that this book holds the key to improving virtually everything *for you*.

Then through you, you will have the greatest potential to improve our world, as only you can.

You might achieve success and reach your goals without applying these lessons. But without doing the inner work I outline within these pages, you may arrive at "success" only to find yourself feeling unfulfilled, overwhelmed, or still dissatisfied: *Is this all there is?*

If this resonates, you're already on the path to something deeper. If it does not, that's okay—stay open. You might be surprised by how these insights can improve your work, your relationships, and most importantly, your entire experience of life.

Let's begin.

WHAT IS INNER LIFE LEADERSHIP?

Simply put, leadership is the ability to work extraordinarily well with and through others, and we do this up, down, across, and both inside and outside of our organization. We also do this at home, as we certainly work with others to maintain a life and a family. As such, you are a leader, and it is your job to direct the attention, talents, and energy of yourself and others well.

The power to create a better tomorrow begins in your mind: in what you choose to focus on, how you respond, and the actions you take. Change your thoughts, and you change your actions, and your results follow suit, as others primarily respond to what it is you do.

This book is about helping you see your own power and authentic influence more clearly. And it is about recognizing the awesome responsibility and privilege of leadership in everyday moments.

Whether you're a CEO running a multibillion-dollar enterprise or currently a stay-at-home parent raising the next generation, leadership is about having a vision for a better tomorrow and taking it upon yourself to enlist others to help make that vision a reality.

Before we explore how you can make your tomorrow better than today, let's begin where all exceptional leadership begins: not in the external world but within ourselves.

This is the essence of Inner Life Leadership.

We often equate leadership with a position or title. People are considered leaders if they manage others or have followers. But that definition is limited, and it misses the true essence of what it means to lead.

A supervisor or boss is not necessarily a leader simply because they hold authority. Regardless of title, role, or followers, anyone can be a leader.

Consider Greta Thunberg[1], who, at 15, skipped school to protest outside Sweden's Parliament and demand the Swedish government actually do something about climate change. She didn't begin with the millions of social media followers she has today; instead, she began with a sign and fliers she handed out to passersby. Ever since, she has inspired climate activists around the world. Age, title, education, or followers have nothing to do with leadership.

Or think of Malala Yousafzai[2], a Pakistani schoolgirl who advocated for girls' education in her region despite personal

1   Charlotte Alter, Suyin Haynes, and Justin Worland, "Time Person of the Year: Greta Thunberg," *Time*, December 30, 2019, https://time.com/person-of-the-year-2019-greta-thunberg/.

2   *Malala's Story*, Malala Fund, accessed May 12, 2025, https://malala.org/malalas-story.

threats. After surviving an assassination attempt by a Taliban gunman as she rode the bus home from school, she "knew she had a choice: she could live a quiet life or make the most of this new life she had been given." With the help of her father, she established the Malala Fund, "a charity dedicated to giving every girl an opportunity to achieve a future she chooses." Her activism led to a global movement for the right to education and made her the youngest-ever Nobel Prize laureate.

There's also Lech Wałęsa[3], a car mechanic and electrician who became a key figure in Poland's Solidarity movement (an anti-communist labor movement that fought for workers' rights) and headed the first independent labor union in a Warsaw Pact country. In 1990, he became the country's first democratically elected president since 1926. His leadership eventually led to the fall of communism in Poland and paved the way for the rise of democracy in Eastern Europe.

Many of history's greatest leaders were regular people who saw something was wrong, and they took action to set it right, often at great personal cost.

Finally, consider Britnie Turner, someone I am blessed to personally know. At 21, Britnie launched Aerial to elevate people and places—but from living out of her car in Nashville, working for free, and learning everything herself. Through grit and vision, she built a thriving real estate development company and social enterprise recognized by *Forbes* as the 6th

---

3   *Lech Wałęsa – Biographical*, The Nobel Prize, accessed May 12, 2025, https://www.nobelprize.org/prizes/peace/1983/walesa/biographical/.

Fastest-Growing Woman-Owned, Women-Led Company in the World.[4]

But Britnie's leadership goes far beyond real estate. After witnessing the horrors of sex trafficking at a young age, she committed her life to ending it. That conviction led her to co-found the *Heal the Heroes* initiative, a year-long program that helps veterans and first responders heal and retrain as Humanitarian Special Operators—heroes on the front lines of anti-human trafficking and disaster response. To date, they have rescued and saved thousands of people.[5]

Your leadership doesn't have to be grand to be significant. Leading yourself and your family to live a life you're proud of is extraordinary. Please don't underestimate the power of living well, treating others with kindness, and striving to be someone worthy of your own highest respect.

It is everything.

My intention with this book is to help you recognize your own power to lead—right here, right now. With every interaction, your presence, words, and actions shape the world around you and become your reality. You impact more people than you realize, and what you do matters.

You lead whenever you do the following:

---

4   "6. Britnie Turner, founder and CEO, Aerial Development Group," *Forbes*, April 21, 2016, https://www.forbes.com/pictures/571901b431358e1869e2a252/6-britnie-turner-founder-/

5   Aerial Recovery, "Disaster Response," *Aerial Recovery*, accessed October 27, 2025, https://aerialrecovery.org/disaster-response.

- Recognize that the world can be better, and you take it upon yourself to create that change, whether or not you hold a title, have authority, or any guarantee of success.

- Realize someone needs to do something about a terrible situation and understand that *you* are, in fact, someone!

- Share your honest thoughts and feelings to truly connect with others, and together, work with them to make tomorrow better than today in some meaningful way.

- Advocate for those who lack a voice, power, or platform, or cannot otherwise advocate for themselves.

- Live your highest values and strive to be a positive force in the lives of others, even, and perhaps most especially, when it is hard to do so.

- Understand that what needs to be done can't often be done alone. So you work to gather the people and resources necessary to respond to the call of leadership, even when you don't feel fully qualified, because most of the time, you won't.

Leadership requires that you not only believe in a better tomorrow but that you also take action to make it better. You don't sit around and complain. You don't stand by in the face of injustice. You don't laugh at jokes that belittle or harm others. You think, act, and communicate in a way that is a living, breathing example of the world you most wish to find.

And to do so, you must do the inner work to know yourself, understand how your thoughts and feelings create your behavior, and recognize how that behavior creates all your results—including your impact on others.

You must learn to listen to your own highest counsel—and act on it.

Inner Life Leadership means doing the work *in here* to create a better world *out there*.

It calls you to be courageous, accountable, and fully yourself—the best, highest, most authentic version of you. And it demands that you want for others what you most want for yourself and your loved ones: health, opportunity, success, fulfillment, and peace.

Welcome! I am so glad you are here.

WHY THIS BOOK?

We are living through a time of extraordinary transformation. Technological advancement, globalization, and the accelerating pace of change are reshaping our world at a speed the likes of which humanity has never seen. The sheer volume of information, disruption, and innovation is relentless, and we're only at the beginning. No one can say with certainty what the next five years will bring or how to best prepare ourselves or our children for such an unknown future.

But amidst this uncertainty, there are things we do know.

Human life has always been hard. This journey, physically, emotionally, and psychologically, is *not* for the faint of heart. We know how the story ends: Everyone grows old and dies. Yet, most of us would not trade this human experience for anything. To be alive is a miracle. To love and be loved makes all the pain worthwhile. To eat food, breathe ocean air, climb a mountain, laugh with a good friend—life, even with all its difficulty and loss, is staggeringly beautiful.

What we live for, perhaps now more than ever, is meaningful connection. Real connection with others is what makes life worthwhile. But to truly connect with others, we must first connect with ourselves. This means we must understand how our early experiences changed us, cultivate a sense of self we respect, and learn how to communicate with clarity, care, and intention. Without doing our inner work, relationships can be confusing, disappointing, and immensely painful. With it, life becomes rich, joyful, and deeply fulfilling.

This Could Be Everything is a call to that inner work. It offers the tools to transform your experience of yourself, because when you change, everything changes. This work is for anyone who wants to feel better, communicate better, and lead better.

WHY NOW? A LEADERSHIP IMPERATIVE

For leaders, this work is not optional. It is the new foundation of effective leadership.

Consider Gen Z, the newest generation in the workforce. They aren't simply looking for jobs. They are seeking purpose, belonging, and growth. They expect transparency, empathy, mental health support, and inclusive cultures. They want to be led by people, not by titles. And they are not afraid to walk away from what doesn't align with their values.

The future of leadership cannot be driven by authority, but it can be driven by authenticity. Leaders must evolve beyond traditional models of command and control. They must be self-aware, emotionally intelligent, and deeply human. Recognition must be personal. Communication must be two-way. Most importantly, leadership must be visible, rooted in purpose, and practiced with humanity.

Gen Z isn't the outlier; they're the leading edge of what most of us now seek: to live and work in meaningful, connected, and authentic ways.

This book is your guide to becoming the kind of leader our world urgently needs. In the first half, you'll learn to trust your instincts, see how your own mind can get in the way of collaboration and influence, and begin shaping a leadership identity grounded in self-understanding and courage.

In the second half, you'll learn how to put that self-understanding into action by communicating with clarity and empathy, building trust with those you lead, and coaching others to become leaders themselves.

WHY TRUST ME?

You deserve to know who is guiding you through this journey and why I am so committed to this cause. I can tell you about my formal education (such as my bachelor's in psychology, master's in applied behavior science coaching and consulting, or diploma in technology, business, and marketing communications), the extensive training I've completed with thought leaders like Tony Robbins, Dr. Joe Dispenza, and Peter Diamandis, or the many publications and presentations I've delivered.

But credentials are merely the price of entry. For well over two decades, I have had the honor of working internationally with C-suite and executive-level leaders. I've spent my days listening to the thoughts, concerns, frustrations, challenges, and aspirations of thousands of senior-level leaders in almost every industry. All this to say, I know the inner life experience of some of our world's best and brightest in a way few others could.

The journey my clients have taken to become ever more effective leaders and achieve whole-life success is the same we each must take, and it begins with going inward to understand ourselves.

This book will bring you the very best of what I have shared with thousands of clients in one-on-one coaching sessions. It is also the work I continue myself, as there is no real end to our individual journeys, only moments and opportunities to be the kind of person and leader we most want and intend to be. On my best days, I live up to my own standards, and on others, well, I fail miserably. And that's okay. Our failures make us human, relatable, and humble; they are there to teach us so we can become better each time.

As Oliver Goldsmith once said, "Our greatest glory consists not in never failing, but in rising every time we fall."[6]

As you read this book, please remember that successful people aren't successful because they rarely fail; they're successful because they consistently seek to learn and advance themselves,

---

6   *Quote Origin: Our Greatest Glory Is Not in Never Falling, But in Rising Every Time We Fall,* Quote Investigator, May 27, 2014, https://quoteinvestigator.com/2014/05/27/rising/

always reaching past their comfort zones, failing frequently, and then they use that feedback to improve what they do next. In this way, there is no such thing as failure.

HOW TO GET THE MOST OUT OF THIS BOOK

As you progress through this book, you'll notice that each chapter builds upon the previous one, so it is useful to read it in order, completing the lessons chronologically.

The following chapters are structured as follows:

Chapter Two: About You and *For* You
In this chapter, I invite you to turn inward. Before we can talk about leadership, we must begin with *you*. Who are you? What are your thoughts and beliefs, and how do you see yourself and the world around you? This internal focus is essential because everything you do as a leader will flow from your inner life. This is the foundation that supports the rest of the book. It is by understanding ourselves more deeply that enables us to better understand all others.

Chapter Three: Becoming More Aware: The Outer Life Trap
In chapter three, I invite you to focus on your inner world by paying more attention to your thoughts and feelings and getting curious about how they affect what you do, how you do it, and the results you obtain. My aim is to help you see how we can each get trapped by overidentifying with the mind and chasing only external success, and how you can shift toward a more intentional inner life. By the end of this chapter, you'll better understand the cost of an outer life focus and gain tools to assess and improve your inner experience.

Chapter Four: The Inner Life Opportunity!

Moving inward, chapter four shows you why cultivating your inner life is essential if you want to enjoy your life, because if you haven't noticed, adult life and leadership tend to offer only problems! In this chapter, I walk you through practical ways to put your inner life first each day, from choosing intentional thoughts to fostering key emotions that support your growth. You'll also learn how to use the Self-Inquiry Tool (SIT) to pause, reflect, and consciously respond instead of reacting to life out of habit.

Chapter Five: Greater Self-Knowledge

Next, I help you deepen your understanding of who you are by exploring how your relationships, memories, and daily patterns shape your self-identity. I guide you through practices to reconnect with the qualities you've always had, clarify your values, and choose the identity you want to embody. This chapter reminds you that you don't need to become someone else—you simply need to remember and reclaim who you truly are.

Chapter Six: Interacting With Others

In chapter six, I show you that how we communicate *is* how we lead. In this chapter, you'll see how every conversation is a chance to connect and uplift. I offer reflections, tools, and a five-question framework to help you become more conscious of how your interactions reflect the leader—and human—you want to be.

Chapter Seven: Trust Is Everything
In this chapter, you'll learn that trust isn't just important—it's actually *everything*. Without trust, you cannot be an effective leader, and you won't build meaningful relationships. By the end of this chapter, you'll understand how trust is built (and broken) through consistent patterns, personal accountability, and the courageous use of "I" language. This chapter is a call to lead with integrity, repair what's been damaged when possible, and recognize that trust is the foundation of everything we care most about.

Chapter Eight: Coaching and Developing Others
In chapter eight, I help you take everything you've cultivated within yourself and turn it outward to develop others. I show you that real leadership means helping people grow by listening deeply, seeing their potential, and offering the right mix of coaching, mentoring, and support. This chapter gives you tools and frameworks to elevate others from where they are to where they could be, starting with one simple mindset: *I want you to win!*

Chapter Nine: Leadership for a New World
In the final chapter, we bring it all together as I invite you to meet this unprecedented moment in human history as an embodied leader. You will recognize that leading in this fast-changing world requires both inner depth *and* outer agility. And you will be given the choice to answer the call: Will you become the kind of leader our future needs? Can you lead from a place that's grounded, conscious, courageous, and—most important—joyfully human?

Each chapter focuses on what I call a *Big Idea*, a critical concept that is essential to effective leadership. Within each chapter, I break down the Big Idea into smaller, easily digestible components that are reinforced by practices that will prompt you to reflect on the lesson, answer a few questions, have a conversation, or apply the idea in the real world, allowing you to not only reflect on the ideas but to actually apply each one in practical ways.

Here's how to use them:

- Think of each practice as a new way of communicating with yourself and with others to test the idea in the real world, your world.
- Test the ideas in various settings, in both your personal and professional life. Give each practice a month or two of solid effort. Then, notice the results.
- Remember that you are experimenting with these ideas to learn, grow, and advance beyond where you are today.

I designed this book to be about the application of ideas, as there is very little new information about how to live a truly successful life. It is only through your own experience in applying these ideas that you will come to know the vast and exponential impact these ideas can have when lived genuinely and consistently.

While reading this book, I encourage you to take pen to paper and write down your thoughts, experiences, or answers to the questions and practices I offer.

Writing your thoughts, answers, and reflections is *extremely useful.*

Numerous studies show that the physical act of writing can deepen your understanding of complex concepts.[7] It requires different parts of the brain to work together, making handwriting engage the brain more fully than merely typing or recording your ideas electronically. Writing allows you to process your experiences more fully, helping you develop more awareness of your inner life and how central it is to everything you care about and all your results *out there.*

The Big Ideas and Practices are designed to let you see your familiar ways of thinking, feeling, and acting. Then, they will invite you to decide how you most want to think, feel, and act!

BIG IDEA #1: THERE IS YOU, AND THERE ARE YOUR THOUGHTS

Are you aware that you have thoughts, but you are not your thoughts? I acknowledge that this concept can be challenging at first, because well, what does that even mean?

First, let's create this distinction between you and your thoughts. Answer yes or no to the following questions.

- Are you aware that you can think a thought? For example: *That jerk just cut me off!*
- Are you also aware that you can think differently? *Whoa, he must be in a hurry,* or *Maybe there's a family emergency.*

---

7   Jonathan Lambert, "Why Writing by Hand Beats Typing for Thinking and Learning," *NPR,* May 11, 2024, https://www.npr.org/sections/health-shots/2024/05/11/1250529661/handwriting-cursive-typing-schools-learning-brain.

- Are you aware that you can have the first thought and notice you feel angry, but also that if you have the second thought, you might feel both concerned and grateful that neither you nor your loved ones are in trouble?
- Are you aware that you can *choose* how you think about a situation?

If you answered yes, brilliant! You understand that you have thoughts, and at the same time, you have some awareness that you are not those thoughts. There is you, and there are your thoughts. You are the one who is aware of them.

If you answered "no" to any of the questions or don't yet grasp this distinction or perhaps disagree with it, that is okay. Keep reading to see what might be here for you.

Here are a few things to keep in mind as you move through this work:

- The work of looking at ourselves can be challenging. It can be hard for me to look at myself because it often makes me feel scared, uncertain, confused, bad, or somewhat disappointed that I am not the person I most hoped to be. If you feel this way, please know you are in good company. As the saying goes, "The truth will set you free, but first, it will piss you off."
- Try to acknowledge the challenge in undertaking this work, as it is intangible and introspective in nature. It is difficult and weird to step outside of our usual thought patterns and get curious about where we place our most precious commodity: our inner attention. *What the*

> *hell am I thinking most days, and is that the life I want to continue?*

- Be kinder to yourself than you ever have been before. I want your inner dialogue to sound something like this: *I'm so proud of you for picking up this book and wanting to learn and grow. You are successful in your very desire to improve. With a touch of levity and humor, I am going to make this inner exploration fun! I wonder how great I can make my own experience of life, and how, by doing so, I might be better with and for others.*

Oliver Wendell Holmes Sr. argued that "every now and then a man's mind is stretched by a new idea or sensation, and never shrinks back to its former dimensions."[8] Keep that in mind, and as you read this book, take some safe risks and see what you can discover.

Success requires only that you get curious and try new ways of thinking and feeling. It involves stepping outside your comfort zone to grow and become more of who you know you are deep within yourself. I believe in you and trust that not only can you manage the discomfort you will feel, you will also be so much better for it!

WHAT THIS BOOK CAN DO FOR YOU

If you apply the ideas presented throughout these pages genuinely and consistently, here's what's likely to happen:

---

8   Oliver Wendell Holmes, "The Autocrat of the Breakfast-Table: Every Man His Own Boswell," The Atlantic Monthly, September 1858, https://www.theatlantic.com/magazine/archive/1858/09/the-autocrat-of-the-breakfast-table-every-man-his-own-boswell/627571/, accessed October 24, 2025.

First, you'll experience a feeling of relief, as if you can stop running, chasing, and endlessly trying to become someone else or get to some better, future moment. You will feel like you are finally enough. You will feel sufficient as you are. You'll realize that there is nowhere to go or get to, and you'll see that both you and this moment are insanely cool right now, exactly as they are.

How great is that?

Soon after, you'll find yourself smiling more, being easier to be around, and accomplishing more with less worry, stress, and effort than you might have ever experienced in your life to date. Relationships will be fun and rewarding, and you will wonder how you ever missed noticing this much joy in everyday events.

There's a lot to be gained.

PRACTICE #1: CONSIDER THE THOUGHT "YOU DON'T HAVE TO BE WHO YOU WERE YESTERDAY."

Simply consider this one thought: *You don't have to be who you were yesterday.*

- Isn't that the most exciting thought you can imagine?
- What would be possible for you if you believed this one thought?
- What freedom would this thought make available to you today?

I don't have to be who I was yesterday is a powerful invitation to transformation. It liberates you from the constraints of the past, which is always filled with limiting beliefs and habitual behaviors. Perhaps you will take that first step toward a long-held dream, mend a strained relationship, or just allow yourself to be happier. The possibilities are endless when you free yourself from the narrative of the past.

CHAPTER TWO

ABOUT YOU AND *FOR* YOU

Take a moment to consider: Who are you? What defines you? Is it your job, your relationships, your values, religion, or politics? Is it what your parents believe(d) about you or what your friends say? Is it who society tells you to be?

These aren't just philosophical questions. They go to the very core of your ability to lead, live well, and make choices that are true to you.

Maybe your mom always wanted you to be a doctor. Perhaps a mentor insists you learn a trade. Maybe society is pressuring you to become a parent. These may all be meaningful paths, and they might even interest you—but the real question is: **What do you want?**

We live in a world that constantly tries to define who we are and who we should be. It's subtle, constant, and might even be well-intentioned. But when we shape ourselves to fit into roles and expectations that don't fully belong to us, we unintentionally create barriers to our own freedom, fulfillment, and authentic success.

So, let's try something different.

Think about someone you deeply admire. What is it about them that earns your admiration? Is it their job title? Their bank account? Their house or their physique?

Or is it something more?

Maybe it's their courage, their kindness, or their integrity. Maybe it's that they've walked their own path—that they've dared to fully be themselves, even when it wasn't easy. Often, the people we admire most are the ones who become most fully themselves.

That's the first essential step in both leadership and life: learning how to be ourselves.

Learning how to be ourselves might sound obvious, except it isn't common. We live in a noisy world, full of people who are eager to tell us who we are or what we should be. But leadership begins when you stop letting others define you and begin listening to yourself: your instincts, your dreams, and your truth.

Most of us are so immersed in external expectations that we don't even realize how much they influence us. It's like asking a fish to notice the water they are swimming in. The fish would probably ask, "What water?"

That's how society works; it surrounds us so completely that we often can't see it. We chase goals, we make decisions, and we live our lives based on how we think we're supposed to, constantly concerned with how others perceive us. We give away our agency without even realizing it.

And when we *do* listen and hear ourselves, we don't often trust what we hear. We doubt our instincts. We question our desires. We suppress our own voice, thinking someone else must know better.

But what if they don't?

What if the most trustworthy voice in your life is your own?

You don't have to live according to someone else's story. You don't have to wear identities that don't fit you, chase goals that don't belong to you, or stay quiet when your soul wants to speak.

Real leadership is freedom. But you must grant this freedom to yourself. And it comes at a cost (psst, the inner work I outline in this book).

Let this chapter be your invitation to start paying more attention to your own thoughts, feelings, instincts, and experience.

This is your life. And you get to live it as you.

Let's keep going.

THE MOMENT OF LEADERSHIP

We all want to be successful, win the approval of others, and be chosen for those limited, top, coveted positions. We work hard to become educated, accomplished, and known as the best at what we do. Unfortunately, success becomes increasingly challenging to define as we progress in life and leadership, particularly as we ascend the organizational ladder and reach the pinnacles of our chosen field. To make matters worse, there is no sure path to achieving it, even if we can clearly define it for ourselves.

As is true in parenthood, there is an inevitable loneliness that comes with being a leader.

Leadership is daunting, and if we have risen through the ranks by being noticed, celebrated, and acknowledged for what we have done, it can feel empty when we finally reach the next level, where there are fewer to no elders left to say what we all still desire to hear: "You're doing a great job!" There can be an uneasy feeling of being untethered, and the illusion of an ultimate authority who could offer solid direction, validation, or approval is just that: an illusion.

- "What should I do?"
- "Why am I not getting any direction, acknowledgment, or validation?"
- "I don't know what 'they' want!"

The transition to leadership can be compared to the transition to parenthood. Although we are not all parents, most of us understand the analogy.

Just as parenting requires deep understanding and acceptance of the responsibility to nurture and guide, effective leadership requires a similar commitment to personal growth and the development of others. This transition from self-awareness to a professional leadership role mirrors the evolution that a parent goes through just after the birth of their first child. Both involve a profound awareness of how their actions and decisions affect others' lives, livelihoods, well-being, and growth.

I remember the first day I was alone with our newborn son. When my husband returned to work, there I was, by myself for the very first time with a six-pound, two-day-old human being. It was a life that I, alone, was responsible for, for the next 10 hours and for at least the next 20 years!

All was well for the first hour while he napped. Then, he awoke: wet, crying—*screaming!* I have never been able to stand the cries of my own children; I suspect this is nature's way of ensuring parents will comfort and care for their babies. I immediately ran over to change him. Picking him up, I felt how fragile his arms and legs were. I was sure I would break them by forcing them into a clean onesie.

And that's when it happened, the moment I became a parent: I stepped back from my baby, afraid, only to realize there was no one else there. No one else was coming. It was entirely up to me. *Oh, my goodness, I am it! I am the only one he has!*

My son looked up at me as if to ask, "You've got this, right?" So, I replied with the only acceptable answer: "Yes, I've got this!"

Then, tears streaming down my face, I thought, *I don't know how to do this! I've never done this before, but I'm the mother you've got, and I will not let you down! I'll figure everything out. I promise. I've got this. I've got you, my beautiful son!*

And just like that, I was a parent. I stopped looking to others to tell me what to do, how to do it, or to validate whether I was doing a good job.

Instead, I turned inward and began trusting my own thoughts, intuition, and judgment.

This transition must also occur when we accept a leadership position: *Okay, these people are now my people. No one can tell me how to be great for them. I must rely upon myself. I must listen to and trust my own judgment. It is my job to serve them. I might not consider myself a strong leader, but I am the one they've got. I can and need to seek advice and counsel from those I admire and trust, but I alone must decide and live with the consequences. This is all on me.*

In both leadership and parenthood, the stakes are incredibly high.

Then the time came when I searched for a potential daycare; it reminded me that, just like in leadership, in parenthood, the ultimate responsibility rested with me. If something as tragic as my child getting hurt, abused, or, worse, dying happened, it wouldn't matter if I had found the greatest daycare in town, paid a great deal of money to hire the best, or vetted them fully. The outcome would be the outcome. Delegating responsibilities doesn't mean I am not responsible for the results. This is all on me. As a leader, the buck stops with me. As a leader, it stops with you.

This is the promise of leadership: to care for and look after our people, to do everything we possibly can to serve them, and to be wholly responsible and accountable for the results.

LEARNING TO TRUST YOURSELF

For well over two decades, I've listened to highly educated, successful professionals in almost every field talk about their goals, dreams, aspirations, frustrations, and challenges. This experience has taught me what really makes someone successful, not just at work but in life, too, like being great with other people, having meaningful relationships, and staying healthy in body and mind.

What I've learned is that there's very little new information on how to live a truly successful life. But it's rarely about needing new information. Rather, it's about our ability to apply the basics *consistently* in real life, especially during a phase I call "the messy middle," between the ages of 30 and 60, when we are dealing with so much between work and family that it is easy for even the best of us to lose our way. We eat too much, drink too much, exercise too little, escape with drugs, porn, cheating, and work, and then damage or lose what we care most about: key relationships and our health.

This loss of direction doesn't happen all at once. It's subtle and cumulative, often beginning when we stop listening to our (highest) selves and start conforming to what we think is expected of us. Before we know it, we've traded authenticity for approval and instinct for external validation.

When we're children, we are naturally ourselves. We wear our favorite purple polka-dot shirt with lime-green pants to school, sing loudly in public, and proudly voice our opinions. But by the time we reach our mid-20s, we often stop questioning what society and our small circle of family, friends, and colleagues believe constitute success. We reach a point where those around us have shaped our thinking so profoundly that we can no longer hear ourselves.

And if we still can hear our own voice, we struggle to trust it. We conform without even realizing we're doing so and wind up believing that this is just the way the world is.

Ralph Waldo Emerson would tell us to listen to the children we used to be. To be successful and happy, we must relearn how to trust ourselves because, as Emerson says, "Great [people] have always done so."[9]

You know more than you give yourself credit for; don't let other people's thoughts make you forget your own.

To honor the confidentiality that is central to my work, every client example shared in this book is a composite. While the situations, challenges, and insights are all drawn from real coaching conversations, no single story belongs to one individual. Instead, each example represents a summation of many clients—sometimes dozens, sometimes hundreds— woven together and told as if it were one person. I've chosen this approach intentionally, to bring key ideas to life in relatable, real-world ways while protecting the privacy and dignity of every client I've worked with. Many of them will read this book, and no one should ever feel exposed, misrepresented, or betrayed.

---

9   Ralph Waldo Emerson, "Self-Reliance," *National Humanities Center*, May 12, 2025, https://nationalhumanitiescenter.org/pds/triumphnationalism/cman/text8/ selfreliance.pdf.

Take Raj, a highly respected executive with a military background and decades of experience leading complex, multibillion-dollar operations. He was the kind of leader others deferred to—steady, strategic, and well trained in every form of high-level leadership. He had sat in every seat, attended every course, and was known as someone who could handle anything.

But even the most seasoned leaders can struggle to trust themselves when it matters most.

Raj's company was preparing for a major merger, one that would redefine the organization's future. On paper, the partnership looked ideal. But behind his calm exterior, Raj had growing concerns—specifically about one of the key people on the other side of the deal. Something wasn't adding up in the way this individual navigated early conversations: the subtle inconsistencies, the too-smooth answers. Raj felt it, but he hadn't named it. Not even to himself.

When we finally sat down to talk, Raj began to share what he *really* thought—that perhaps this person wasn't who he said he was. That if Raj was right, they were about to bring a problem directly into the heart of their business. As he spoke, I realized this was the first time he was saying any of this out loud.

I asked, "Have you shared this with your CEO or your partners?"

He shook his head and said quietly, "No. I don't know if I would share this."

Why? Because somewhere along the way, Raj had learned what so many senior leaders are taught: Your feelings are not data, and your doubts are not welcome in the boardroom. But they are. They always are. Because beneath our polished logic and PowerPoint presentations, our finest instrument is still our instinct—the quiet, persistent voice that sees something before it's visible and feels something before it's confirmed.

Yet, how often do we notice something, feel it deeply, and say nothing?

In Raj's earlier leadership roles, conversations with superiors were often shaped more by hierarchy than honesty. The unspoken expectation was to have answers, not questions— to manage concerns internally, not voice them openly. Vulnerability was equated with weakness, and instincts were often sidelined. So when I asked why he hadn't shared his unease about the partnership, he paused, then said thoughtfully, "I wasn't fully aware of how concerned I am by that one executive team member. I don't trust him, but I don't really know why just yet. I need to think about this and talk to Tony and get his read. I don't know if I'm off or if something else is happening."

This is so common among senior leaders. We notice things, feel them, sense them in subtle ways—but we don't always know how to name them or trust them. We're trained to lead with logic and certainty, not with intuition and unfinished thoughts.

Raj began to more fully tune into the quiet signals he had long been conditioned to dismiss. He began to trust not just what he *knew*, but also what he *felt*.

That shift became important during a critical meeting with equity partners. The company was preparing to greenlight a major move, one that everyone else seemed eager to finalize. But Raj felt the timing was wrong. The pressure felt manufactured, and the rationale didn't fully hold. His body knew it before his words did.

Rather than stay silent, Raj started with a peer, saying, "This doesn't seem to make sense right now," and shared what was behind his hesitation.

To his surprise, the peer replied, "I think you're right. We've been under pressure to move forward, but honestly, I've had the same concerns."

Together, they brought their perspective to the CEO and board advisors. That single act of candor changed the course of a major decision. The team reconsidered, delayed the move, and avoided what could have been a costly misstep.

And it all began with Raj learning to more fully trust and speak the subtle truths he had once overlooked—even within himself.

Despite his vast leadership experience, Raj (like most of us) needed to *hear* the subtlety of his own thoughts, feelings, and instincts and he needed to validate them as important information. Then, and this is critical, he needed to act upon them. The ability to do this sounds obvious, and yet it isn't. The ability to hear ourselves in a noisy world, with powerful personalities, one rapidly being changed by AI, is more critical than we know.

Now imagine the newest hire in your organization. They're fresh out of college and have spent the last four years of their life learning the latest innovations and strategies in the industry. At the next team meeting, they're dying to share their perspective. But they're afraid they'll look foolish or be dismissed by senior members of the team, so they keep quiet. Those ideas, shaped by a skilled expert, are now lost to the company because the new hire was afraid to share them.

Like Raj, we are all on a personal journey of learning to hear ourselves more fully and to learn to what extent we can (and must) act upon what it is we know. This successful experience reminded Raj of the impact of leading more authentically and that he can and must trust himself more.

Whether you're a seasoned professional like Raj or just out of college, it's crucial that you pay more attention to your *own* thoughts and feelings.

How often do you act upon what you *know*? If I excel at anything, it is in helping people listen to, trust, and act on their inner knowing more than they currently allow themselves to do.

To gauge how much you trust yourself, consider the following:

- In meetings and group conversations, how often do you say to yourself, "That's exactly what I was thinking. Why didn't *I* say it?"
- After completing a project, do you often feel the urge to kick yourself for neglecting something you *knew* you should have done (as that oversight has now come back to bite you)?

- Is there someone you *already know* you need to fire (or move to another part of the organization) but have yet to do so?

- Is there a challenging conversation you *know* you need to have? How long do you suspect you'll wait before actually having it?

The concept of self-trust is straightforward. Naturally, we should trust ourselves! Many of us are successful, educated, and experienced professionals, possibly holding senior leadership positions. However, as an executive in one of my sessions remarked, "Acting on my inner knowing is harder than it sounds!" Indeed, it is.

Applying what you already know is more challenging than simply knowing it, but that's where the real work lies. For instance, regarding diet, exercise, and health, isn't it true that you likely know two or three key actions that, if you did them consistently, would enhance your well-being and significantly contribute to your long-term health and vitality? The crux of the matter isn't about knowing what to do but consistently acting on that knowledge.

BIG IDEA #2: LEARN TO TRUST YOURSELF

To make your tomorrow better than today, you must *act upon* your own best thinking. And to do so, you first need to learn to hear it. Here's how to get started:

PRACTICE #2: A FIVE-MINUTE SELF CHECK-IN

Take five minutes, and if you can, get outside and go for a walk or otherwise change your environment. As you walk, pay attention to what comes to your mind: What thoughts? What feelings? For example, you might notice that you feel bad, and when you follow that feeling more, you realize that you are concerned about an interaction you had earlier in the day: *I feel bad because I failed to check in with John after that difficult conversation.* With this greater awareness, you might advise yourself, *I should really check in with him.*

Now, find an opportunity to act on this heightened awareness of your thoughts and feelings: *I'm going to call John and check in.*

Act and notice the result:

- How did your call with John go?
- How did it affect him? What was the impact on your relationship, the task, or business?
- Were your instincts accurate?
- What did you learn by acting more on your own thoughts and feelings?

REFLECT: TIME FOR YOU

At this stage in your life, with everything occurring in the world and the vast implications for the global economy, your industry, and your business, few things get to be about *you*— how you are feeling or really doing, deep inside of yourself.

It is likely that your job requires you to give to everyone else: vision, strategy, answers, time, attention, information, approval, feedback, coaching, encouragement, validation, and confidence. In order to perform and be successful, it seems everyone around you either wants or needs something *from you.* You focus on others all day at work. Then, if you are a spouse, parent, child to aging parents, and/or volunteer in your community, you continue this focus on others throughout much of your personal life.

When is your life ever about you?
Steve Jobs used to walk with his coach, Bill Campbell[10], on Sundays, which he used as time for himself—time to reflect, talk freely, hear himself think, gain perspective, and focus himself. If you don't currently have someone like Bill in your life, please use this book as one way to quiet the demands of the world and make time for you, the human being behind your many responsibilities.

What is one thing you most want *for yourself this year?*

Perhaps you lack the passion you once had, and you really do want to be a more inspiring and optimistic person. Or maybe your health has taken a back seat for far too long, and you now want to live up to your own highest standard for your weight, strength, or stamina.

Whatever it is, name one deeply personal goal you have *for yourself*—a goal that if you advanced toward it, *you* would feel amazing, thereby allowing you to sustain yourself well for everyone else who needs and draws upon you.

You have permission to be in your own life!

At first, this may sound obvious. You might think: *Of course, I get to be in my own life—it's my life.* But is it? How much of your

---

10   Eric Schmidt, Jonathan Rosenberg, and Alan Eagle. Trillion Dollar Coach: The Leadership Playbook of Silicon Valley's Bill Campbell. New York: Harper Business, 2019.

life is truly based on what *you* want? And how much is shaped by what you think you're *supposed* to do?

So many of us were taught that being selfish is wrong. But Inner Life Leadership asks you to be selfish in the best way: to take exceptional care of yourself as you can never truly advance, support, or encourage others if you haven't first extended these same courtesies to yourself.

I want you to be selfish and focus at least some of your energy and inner attention on something important to you, deep inside of yourself. When I ask this of my clients, many express wanting the following:

- I want to feel more peace, to be able to be more present.
- I want to be able to enjoy my life and current success more than I do.
- I want to feel healthy, lean, fit, and strong, to be proud of how well I take care of myself.
- I would love to complete _____ project (whether personal or professional).
- I want to devote more time and attention to _____ (learning a new skill, developing a side business, traveling, being a better leader, spouse, parent, or friend).

Your one deeply personal goal should be exciting and life-giving. It should resonate with who you are. It may not make sense to others, and that's okay.

One of my clients decided he wanted a day free of meetings, so he established that boundary: he simply was not available on Fridays unless the issue was both urgent and something only he could address. He has largely succeeded in this, and he's not troubled on the rare occasions when avoiding a Friday meeting isn't possible.

Another client decided she was going to be "that fit woman," so even when her schedule is packed with travel, she finds the hotel gym and completes her weekly workouts, no matter how tired she feels. Another walks with her spouse every morning for connection and health. One who finds cooking therapeutic prepares a gourmet meal at least once a week. And yet another shared that he simply wants to floss every night, because doing so helps him feel he's living up to his own highest standard of self-care.

Your personal goal may seem small, boring, or even silly. It might feel scary, daunting, or incredibly selfish. There's no need to judge. Just acknowledge the one thing you would most love for yourself this year, something important to you, one aspect of your life you want to protect and prioritize, just for you.

WHAT YOU MOST WANT

You do so much for everyone else. Focusing on one deeply personal goal can be grounding, offering a consistent space that is about you and *for* you, set apart from an otherwise demanding schedule and constant responsibilities to others.

Paradoxically, the act of focusing on yourself will make you better *for them.*

For example, my personal goal is to thoroughly enjoy my life today. Having lost both of my parents more than a decade ago, I understand how quickly everything we cherish can be taken from us. Tomorrow is not guaranteed, so I want to savor today while still striving for an even better tomorrow.

To live this goal, I plan my week in a way that supports what matters most to me. I aim to serve my clients well, move important business projects forward, stay healthy, and enjoy meaningful time with my husband, our two kids, and our two dogs.

This planning has become a favorite ritual: Hot coffee in hand, early Sunday morning before anyone else is awake, I review all commitments, priorities, and deliverables, both personal and professional. I schedule my workouts (yoga, strength training with my kids, or hikes with our dogs). I set small weekly goals, like drinking more water or finally painting the deck. I even add rewards like a movie with my kids to motivate myself through the things I resist, like reviewing financials.

One of the things I do to ensure I enjoy each day is to make sure there's always something on the calendar that's just for me. Whether it's time to read, get outside, or connect with a friend, these moments refill my energy and keep me aligned with what matters.

When I take time to intentionally create a week I love, I take care of my happiness. And when I'm happy, I'm great for others.

Now it's your turn. **What is your one personal goal?**

As you reflect on this one goal that is just for you, begin to envision it fully. Grab your journal and take a few minutes to explore:

- Write your one personal goal: *"What I most want for myself this year is _____."*
- Now, write down why you want it: *"This goal is important to me because _____."*
- Finally, identify what you believe you will experience when you achieve this goal: excitement, contentment, peace, energy, freedom, ease, flow, satisfaction, fulfillment, or perhaps a quiet inner pride that you truly are the person and professional you want to be.

So far in this chapter, you've given yourself permission to be in your own life and identified one deeply personal goal that matters most to you this year. This is cause for celebration!

Now, let's take this a step further and explore how shifts in your inner world will shape the success you create in your outer one.

INNER AND OUTER OUTCOMES

Most of us overlook or are unaware of the integral relationship between our inner and outer lives. Let me explain. If you achieve a change in your outer life but it fails to improve how you feel inside (in your inner life), you may quickly become disillusioned, dissatisfied, and confused. For example, you might lose weight, earn more money, finally marry, have children, receive the big promotion, or close the deal of the century, but even then, problems still arise and sometimes new ones you didn't anticipate are created.

At what point do these achievements lead to fulfillment, contentment, and the peace we seek?

When we want something, we typically only think about our outer lives. We want more success, money, a new role, or relationship.

But what we actually want is two things: **A change in our outer life *and* a change in our inner life.**

If we're honest, most of our outer pursuits are driven by a desire to feel something different on the inside.

A few years ago, I started working with a coach who asked me a simple but confronting question: "What do you want?" I gave him a vague answer, avoiding the real question. But he wouldn't let it go.

"No," he said. "What do you really want—financially, professionally, personally?" So I threw out the biggest income number I could imagine, because who doesn't want more money? The number was so large, it felt absurd, even a little embarrassing to say out loud. I could not imagine how it would ever be possible. But he took it seriously.

"Great," he said. "Now let's build the inner infrastructure that can hold that."

I didn't fully understand what he meant at the time, but I trusted him. I set that massive financial goal. And to my surprise, I hit it. It felt incredible. Then I set an even bigger goal. I hit that too.

By the third year of doing this, I had achieved more than I once believed possible. And yes, I had built the inner capacity to hold that success: the confidence, capacity, and discipline required. But even with all that, honestly, my daily life didn't feel all that different. My mind merely focused on the new challenges that having money brought.

The outer changes were not sufficient to what I really wanted: greater peace. It seems that I should have been more specific!

The truth is I felt overwhelmed at this next level: What does one do with extra money? I didn't know how to invest because I had never had extra money to do so. I now had another full-time job: educating myself on investing and making sure I didn't make a mistake and lose it all. It was scary and stressful.

What I had really wanted was to feel successful, secure, and to be able to relax. I wanted to feel more *myself* in my own life. And that's what so many of us are really seeking.

We want to feel alive. We want to feel joy, freedom, love, purpose, *ease!*

That insight shifted everything. I came to understand that we're often trying to create change on two levels at once:

An outer life that reflects our goals and values
and
An inner life that gives us the feelings we most deeply crave.

Most of us neglect the latter, assuming it comes with the former. It does not, unless we have also learned how to foster those feelings along the way.

Success, in its deepest sense, is about creating a life that feels on the inside the way we dream of feeling. That's the work we're doing here together: one Big Idea and Practice at a time!

Return to what you wrote when exploring your one personal goal, and answer the following for yourself:

- What tangible, objectively measurable outer outcome do I most want (e.g., a new job, more money, a life partner, a healthier body)?
- What intangible, subjectively measurable inner outcome do I most desire (e.g., more satisfaction, connection, joy, peace; less stress, angst, loneliness, negativity, frustration)?

Many people spend their lives chasing an outer change to fix how they feel inside. But it cannot be done. Isn't that a relief? Now you can do the work that actually will make a difference.

MAKE IT REAL

As you focus on your one personal goal, take a moment to envision it fully. How would it feel to be living in alignment with your highest standards in this area of your life? What emotions would you experience daily: peace, energy, satisfaction, freedom?

Now think of someone who already lives this goal with ease.

- How do you think they see themselves?
- What thoughts likely guide their decisions?
- If they were in your shoes, what's one action you think they'd take today?

Use this person as a mental guide to remind you of who you are, as those we admire merely show us who we are and want to be.

Before anything else, you must put yourself in your own life. Give yourself permission to want what you want and to take one meaningful step toward its realization today. You deserve to witness yourself becoming who you truly are.

This might be signing up for that run club or course, researching a new company, or calling a colleague. It doesn't need to be big. Even one action creates momentum and gives you evidence that you deserve your own self-esteem.

Years ago, I hired my first executive coach. He charged $400 an hour, an amount so far beyond what I could afford at the time that it felt absurd. I was in my twenties, just starting out, and every instinct told me it was too much. But I couldn't stop thinking about the way he lived. He coached senior leaders early in the morning and late at night, across time zones, and then spent his days with his three young kids, taking them to the park, being present for their lives. He wasn't commuting for hours, racing between meetings, or burning out in a corner office. He had created a life of impact and connection on his own terms.

That, to me, was success—a life well lived. I knew I wanted something like it for myself. So I hired him, even though I had to put it on a credit card. I did it because I wanted to peek into the thinking that allowed him to live that way. I needed to hear how he made decisions, what he focused on, and what he believed, because I knew if I could adopt that mindset, I could begin building a similar life.

And I did. Over time, that one bold decision reshaped everything. By the time my children were born, I had set up my work to mirror what I had once only imagined. I coached early and late, across time zones, so I could be fully present with my kids during the day. Even now, I pick them up from school, attend every basketball game, hockey tournament, and film project, and I still get to collaborate with extraordinary leaders and organizations.

More recently, I made a similar move in another area of my life: my health. I hired a personal trainer who looked and lived the kind of strength and vitality I wanted for myself. I told her, "I know how to eat and train, but I struggle to apply what I know. I want to understand how you think."

She shared one insight that made the entire investment worth it. She said, "I believe I deserve to feel good."

Wait, what? What a novel idea. That was a thought I had never fully considered for myself.

She went on to explain, "After baseball, when my kids ask for something fun, like the rare occasion of stopping for ice cream at a fast-food place, I'll get one for them, but not for myself. Not because I can't, but because I deserve to feel great. If I have the ice cream, I know I won't feel good. I'll break out, my energy will crash, and I'll feel sluggish. So I go home and eat something that's satisfying and makes me feel amazing."

Her thinking was so different from mine. I used to think, *I should be able to enjoy an ice cream with my kids,* and sometimes I do. But usually, I'd wish I hadn't. I saw how my thinking made it a sacrifice.

But she wasn't thinking in terms of sacrifice at all. She believed she deserved something better, something that truly made her feel good, long after the moment had passed.

That one new thought changed my world.

Now, her thoughts have become my own: *I deserve to feel good. What would make me feel great today?*

Often the answer is something that supports my health: getting in a workout, drinking a glass of water, going for a walk, or getting to bed earlier. The shift isn't just in behavior, but in identity. I'm becoming someone who makes decisions from a place of self-worth and self-respect.

If the ideas in this book challenge you, you're not alone. They've challenged me, too, and the thousands of clients I've coached. But with each intentional thought, the life you want is possible.

You are not bound by who you were yesterday. Every moment offers a new opportunity to choose thoughts and actions that align with who you truly are and want to be. Congratulations on taking this time for yourself, to connect with what matters most to you.

Next, we'll venture inward to explore how your inner dialogue shapes your reality.

This is how you master your inner life and elevate every other part of it.

CHAPTER THREE

BECOMING MORE AWARE: THE OUTER LIFE TRAP

What's it like to live inside your mind these days?

Is it fun in there? Peaceful? Do you revel in solitude as much as you enjoy social settings? Or is your mind often filled with bad feelings, anxiety, and disturbing thoughts? If so, welcome to the human experience!

Isn't it sad how a single email or glance in the mirror can ruin your day? Or how your mind can bother you so much that you can't sleep at night? Does it feel like your mind often drives you crazy? If so, isn't it interesting that it can drive *you* crazy?

Many of our thoughts are critical, negative, and rooted in fear. These thoughts can repeat endlessly inside our minds, sometimes for years. That's why Big Idea #3 is so important: *You Are Not Your Mind*. Let's unpack what this really means and how knowing this can shift everything.

BIG IDEA #3: YOU ARE NOT YOUR MIND

When we allow our minds to run the show, we can easily get in trouble, as there is no shortage of thoughts that will entertain, distract, and scare us. The endless mental dialogue can consume all our inner attention, making us lost in thought. Although physically present, we seem a million miles away or appear completely self-absorbed because we are: All of our attention is focused internally. This internal focus is often held captive by fearful and critical thoughts about what we believe we need to feel better than we do right now. What I find ironic is that these thoughts are part of why so many of us feel bad!

To follow your mind's endless parade of thoughts is to live a nightmare.

If we want to severely punish another human being, what do we do? Put them in solitary confinement. For most people, being left alone with only their own mind is extremely uncomfortable, if not downright torturous. Don't you ever wonder what it is inside of ourselves that we just can't seem to endure?

Step back and take note of your mind's bothersome ways.

Take a seat, grab some popcorn, and watch how your mind parades an endless array of scary thoughts to draw your attention away from this moment: Who am I now? How will I survive, get ahead, win? How can I protect what I have built? Are others happier or succeeding more than I am? How can I not embarrass myself? Do others see me the way I want to be seen? Do I even matter?

When we follow our thoughts, we are not present.

Consider the following examples.

- You attend an important meeting and are so concerned with how you are coming across, what others think of you, and how to get what you need that you fail to notice what is happening for others or really pay attention to what they most want and need.
- A friend loses a parent. You feel bad and awkward, so you share condolences but otherwise avoid the topic.
- A colleague shares a recent success, but because it threatens your self-worth, you say little and begin avoiding them.
- You crave validation and recognition from superiors or family but never stop to recognize their need for the same.

Sadly, for most of us, our personal concerns and fears consume much of our lives. For example, I can't see you, because I am so busy looking for and trying to find myself and then looking to see if you see me. I falsely believe these thoughts and fears are mine when, in fact, they are universal and, therefore, impersonal.

This is the same inner life that almost everyone is living.

Observe your incessant mind. Notice how thoughts cascade through your awareness, pulling you away from the present moment. Rather than fleeing into distraction or trying to control your thoughts (which can't really be done) and the feelings they stir up, simply let them be. Just watch. In *The*

Power of Now[11], Eckhart Tolle likens the mind to a small child—constantly chattering, demanding attention, inventing dramas. His point is not to shame the mind, but to help us realize we don't need to take every thought so seriously. Like a child throwing a tantrum, your mind may yell, replay fears, rehearse failures, and invent futures that haven't happened. Watch it with gentle curiosity, not identification.

- What thoughts does your mind replay most often?
- What fears does it dwell on and like to rehearse?

I'm asking you to become more fully aware of where you invest your most precious commodity: your internal attention. What you choose to think about and how those thoughts make you feel. Yes, feelings can lead to thoughts and thoughts to feelings, but let's not worry about what comes first as both matter for our purposes.

What collection of thoughts do you have on repeat?

What if, as you notice them now, you can think of them only as the antics of a small child and know there is nothing particular for you to do about any of them?

- Might that change your entire experience of life?
- Might that allow you to finally be free to connect with others and do what is needed to best improve the moment right in front of you?

If your experience is anything like mine, each day my thoughts seem to have less of a hold on me. Thinking positive thoughts

---

11   Eckhart Tolle, *The Power of Now: A Guide to Spiritual Enlightenment* (New World Library, 2004).

over negative ones can be helpful. However, there is enormous peace when I don't give my thoughts all that much attention. I simply notice them as I might (bad) background music—a little bothersome, but something I can easily tune out.

There are even days when I fully experience how my thoughts have nothing to do with me, as most of them were handed to me by society and those who raised me; I can see they are not mine at all. Better still, I can see most of them are embarrassingly self-absorbed, silly, and downright ridiculous.

Previously, I so often took my thoughts as reality and then focused on what I needed to do to fix how I felt. Now I simply disengage from the thought and realize that, more often than not, I don't need to do anything about it, because nothing actually needs fixing. I then have the presence to deal with what is occurring: responding to my child, seeking clarity in a business negotiation, or noticing how another person is hurting.

I am most effective when I don't act on my thoughts but rather act out of inspiration. I can tell the difference because my thoughts tell me I should or need to do something, usually out of fear of what will occur if I don't; whereas actions that rise out of inspiration always feel natural, spontaneous, and exciting. They arise out of the present and are based in love and a desire to serve. They expect and need nothing in return.

I also experience the greatest creative freedom and corresponding business success on the days I no longer take the content of my mind all that seriously. I cannot do this every day or for very long. However, I am encouraged by my own progress. What used to upset or consume my attention only a couple of years ago now barely registers.

Of course, there are times when thinking is necessary, like when solving a problem, planning a project, or organizing something that involves several people. I try to engage my thinking mind when thinking is needed, and when it's not, I work to let go of thoughts and return to presence.

You are NOT your habitual thoughts and feelings. You have simply rehearsed many of these for years. I want you now to become aware of what you have rehearsed.

For example, for many years, my internal attention focused on my weight, specifically the 10–20 pounds I wanted and was told to lose. Most women know this ridiculousness and how consuming and painful it can be. The amount of energy I put into worrying about that extra weight could have been used to further develop my business or invest in relationships. Instead, because those thoughts had become part of my daily reality, I didn't question them. It wasn't until I read *The Beauty Myth*[12] by Naomi Wolf that I realized what a vast and unnecessary distraction this was, so I started focusing my mind on things that *mattered*. Ironically, the additional weight that made me miserable for years disappeared as soon as I stopped obsessing about it.

In coaching senior leaders, I've found that we often overlook how significantly our thoughts and feelings, our inner life, shape our overall experience:

---

12   Naomi Wolf, *The Beauty Myth: How Images of Beauty Are Used Against Women* (Chatto & Windus, 1990).

- Your thoughts and feelings drive everything you do and how you do it.

- Your thoughts and feelings dictate what you see (or fail to see) as possibilities and choices for yourself, your family, your team(s), and your business(es).

- Your thoughts and feelings drive your behavior, which in turn drives the state of all your relationships and the results you obtain (or fail to obtain) in your personal *and* professional life.

It sounds obvious when you read it. But it's easier to see in others.

Take the CEO who's consumed by a potential acquisition. He's stressed, doesn't sleep well, and starts snapping at his executive team. He doesn't intend to, but his preoccupation colors every interaction. His team, as a result, grows more cautious and risk-averse, just when he needs them at their most energized and innovative.

We've all seen it. The link between a person's internal life and external results is often immediate and profound.

But what about you?

How do your thoughts and feelings shape the way you lead, communicate, and connect with the world around you?

PRACTICE #3: THREE THOUGHTS

- Write down three thoughts you had this morning.
- Notice if those are thoughts you think often, perhaps every morning.

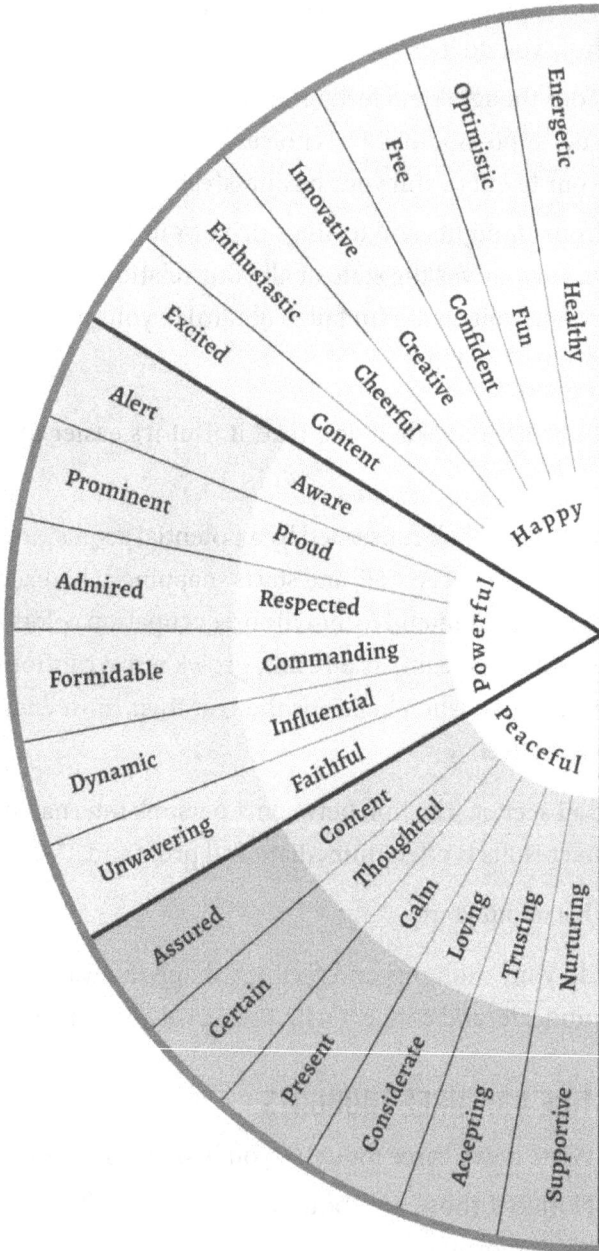

Energetic
Healthy
Optimistic
Free
Fun
Innovative
Confident
Enthusiastic
Creative
Excited
Cheerful
Alert
Content
Aware
Prominent
Proud
Admired
Respected
Happy
Formidable
Commanding
Powerful
Influential
Dynamic
Faithful
Peaceful
Unwavering
Content
Thoughtful
Assured
Calm
Loving
Certain
Trusting
Nurturing
Present
Considerate
Accepting
Supportive

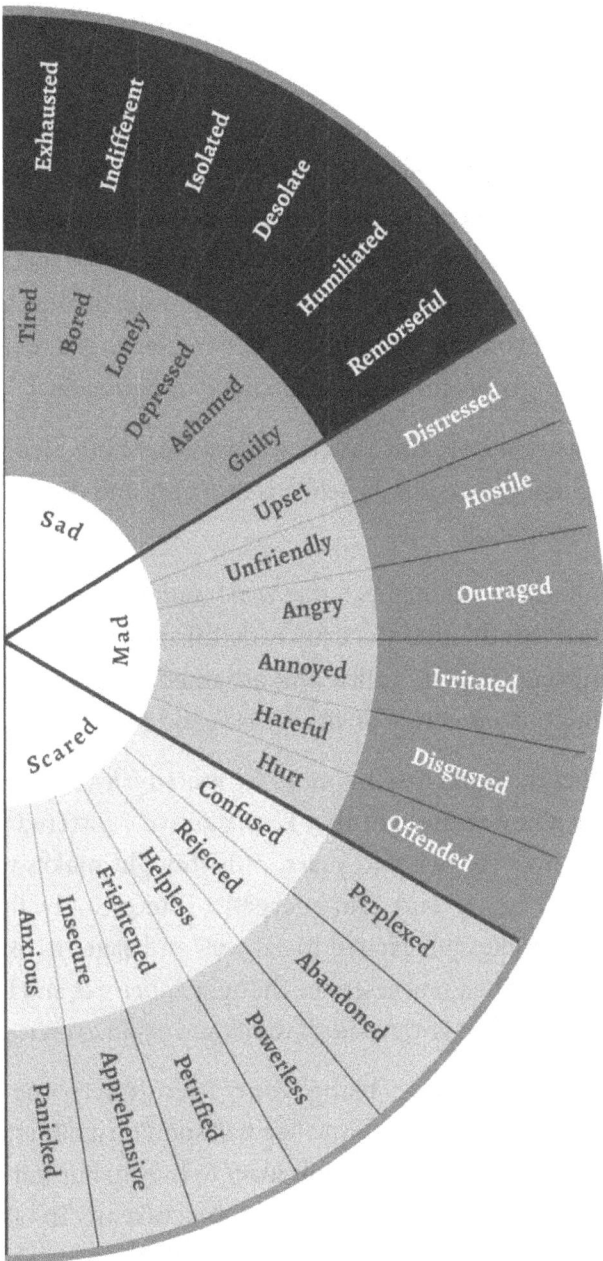

The feeling wheel showing categories of emotions. The central core includes: Sad, Mad, Scared.

Sad section (outer rings): Tired, Bored, Lonely, Depressed, Ashamed, Guilty, Exhausted, Indifferent, Isolated, Desolate, Humiliated, Remorseful

Mad section (outer rings): Upset, Unfriendly, Angry, Annoyed, Hateful, Hurt, Distressed, Hostile, Outraged, Irritated, Disgusted, Offended

Scared section (outer rings): Confused, Rejected, Helpless, Frightened, Insecure, Anxious, Perplexed, Abandoned, Powerless, Petrified, Apprehensive, Panicked

- Read the three thoughts aloud and then capture how they make you feel.

Many of us struggle to identify our emotions. We often stop at broad labels like mad or sad, without being able to pinpoint exactly what we're feeling. I've included a Feelings Wheel in this chapter to help you identify your feelings more specifically. The Feelings Wheel helps by offering a prompt of more specific words, so you can move from a general feeling, like mad, to something more precise, like offended or outraged.

To illustrate how this practice works, here are a couple of thoughts I noticed in myself this morning and the emotions they brought up.

One of my first thoughts today was *I should be further ahead.* I've had this thought since my early thirties, and it makes me feel upset, anxious, guilty, and ashamed. These are terrible feelings that often ruin an otherwise good day.

Another thought I had this morning was *I am lean and healthy.* This is a newer thought that I have actively fostered within myself over the last two years. This thought makes me feel good, excited, proud, and energetic. Interestingly, this one thought makes me excited to eat well and eager to exercise. Previously, I had rehearsed the thought *I am tired*, and it made me want to eat less-than-ideal foods and avoid exercise.

The goal here is to bring your attention to the inner environment you live in *now*. We will soon turn our attention to the inner environment you *want* to live in, but not before you notice the inner environment you currently inhabit and have no doubt rehearsed for months, if not years.

MORE ON INNER AND OUTER LIFE

We addressed inner and outer outcomes as you identified your one personal goal for yourself this year.

Now, let's build on this further.

I want to clarify the distinction between inner life and outer life as I intend it.

We constantly interact with two environments: our outer world, the people, events, and circumstances around us.

Our inner life includes:

- our thoughts,
- how those thoughts make us feel, and
- our physical sensations.

This inner life is deeply shaped by our personal history. It dictates how we interpret and experience each moment, often without our awareness. Childhood taught us what to expect from people, power, illness, success, and money. How these were handled in our early environment became our unconscious norm, silently influencing our beliefs, our expectations, and how we navigate the world today.

We live in a body and feel its signals of pain, hunger, and fatigue, and our emotional responses and interpretations are filtered through the lens of our past. This is how we drag our personal history into the present. The child who was neglected may still seek constant approval, even as a confident executive. The child who was punished or shamed may still feel undeserving of ease or success, regardless of how much they've achieved.

Without awareness of our personal histories and the unconscious norms they created within us, we carry these patterns into every present moment. They shape what we notice (or fail to notice), how we interpret others' actions, and what we believe is possible. We unknowingly recreate the same life experience, relationship dynamics, and internal struggles, even in completely new environments. This is why no amount of external success can resolve what remains unexamined internally.

- *I still feel powerless.*
- *I don't feel like I deserve success.*
- *It is my job to ensure others are happy.*

Awareness is the turning point. It allows us to see our history not as a script to repeat but as context we can grow beyond. Becoming conscious of our inner landscape is essential, because it shapes everything: how we think, how we feel, how we act, and how we lead.

On the other hand, our outer life comprises what we outwardly express and do, anything that could be captured on video. It's the part of us that is observable to others. Of course, what others can see represents only a fraction of the vastness within us. Others cannot know our fears, insecurities, values, or motivations.

Our outer life includes:

- what we say and how we say it (such as our choice of words and tone of voice);

- nonverbal behavior (eye contact, facial expressions, and body language); and
- the clothes we wear, the things we own, and what we share about ourselves online and in real life.

Like yin and yang, your inner and outer life are intrinsically related. Each shape and is shaped by the other. But your inner life leads and when it is out of balance, your outer life will follow suit.

Perhaps you wake up with a stiff neck because you're still unsettled from an issue at work. Internally, you replay the situation over and over, each loop intensifying your concern. You're not just reacting to what happened; you're reacting through the lens of your past. Perhaps you learned early on that conflict is unsafe, so you failed to address a matter early and now the problem has grown. This internal stress, coupled now with physical neck pain, and internal reprimand spills into your outer life, showing up as tension or irritability with family members and colleagues who have nothing to do with the situation.

Or maybe constant concern for your children or aging parents weighs heavily on you. You find yourself short-tempered and stretched thin. Everyone expects you to deliver, to hold it all together. As the oldest child, you learned to be the responsible one. Now you're stuck in a cycle of always giving but you're unable to receive. You support everyone else but often feel resentful and deeply alone.

You might be grappling with aging, noticing weight gain, disliking your appearance, and feeling disconnected from yourself. What once worked to manage your body no longer does, and underneath the frustration is an old belief: that your worth is tied to how you look. Maybe this belief took root in college, as you watched how many opportunities were afforded to those who were physically attractive. Now those same feelings resurface. You avoid being on camera, decline social invitations, and quietly retreat. You feel embarrassed, exhausted, and far from the life you want to live.

These examples reveal how personal history shapes present experience. Without awareness, we drag the past into every present moment, unknowingly recreating the same emotional reality.

THE OUTER LIFE TRAP

Over the last two decades, I've worked one-on-one with some of the world's most educated, successful, and seasoned professionals. Despite their accomplishments, I've noticed that even the best can find themselves stuck, unable to reach new levels of effectiveness, satisfaction, and fulfillment in their personal and professional lives.

This stagnation stems from a habit of thought—a persistent and limited way of thinking that is primarily, if not exclusively, focused on their outer life.

To understand what brought someone to executive coaching, I often start with a straightforward question: "Why are we speaking?"

"Well, apparently, I'm an asshole." This is an answer I've heard countless times, sometimes verbatim and sometimes couched in more polite words. "Are you an asshole?" I inquire. We both laugh. "Yes, I suppose I can be."

"Hey, me too. We all can be. Here is your coaching advice: Stop doing that." Again, we both laugh.

We then get to work, exploring everything impacting the executive's life: the challenges of leading in a global marketplace, the politics playing out at the senior leadership level, and the resulting lack of trust, engagement, and desired results throughout their organization.

And this is to say nothing about their personal life and its complexities, which might include raising children, caring for aging parents, or coping with divorce, illness, and death.

To get to the heart of their challenges, I'll ask, "What is actually happening within you?"

The answers to this question vary greatly, but the essence is always what is happening within each of us: Our personal histories are impacting our present reality.

All the messages we received in childhood, the self-identity we solidified in young adulthood, the methods we developed to protect ourselves and now unconsciously rely upon to mask our insecurities, fears, and limitations—these are always playing out externally.

Some leaders will say something along the lines of "I don't suffer fools gladly."

I'll ask, "Who are the fools?" and we'll talk about the performance of the people they lead. Perhaps they need to be fired or moved into another role, because they won't be successful or able to take the organization where it needs to go.

My response here is to impress upon my client that the remaining people are your people and the job is to serve, nurture, and advance them. They must ensure their people are successful and have every opportunity to do their best and highest work. Executives no longer get to think of any of them as fools.

This leads to other questions I often ask: "How do you wish you could handle yourself and the challenges of your executive role? Who do you want to be?"

While the specifics of each answer vary, their underlying meanings are similar:

> I want greater self-control. I want to stop getting so frustrated and impatient. I often feel angry, and it affects all my relationships. I can be rude at work. I'm short with my family. I don't sleep well. I carry on conversations in my head. I am rarely present. I am out of shape and exhausted. I wish I could lead with greater maturity, intelligence, quiet confidence, and ease. I want to feel more peace, health, excitement, and fulfillment. It would be incredible to enjoy my life and current success far more than I do.

Research conducted by the Leadership Circle organization[13], involving more than 155,000 leaders across over 25,000 organizations, 246 countries, and 65 industries, found that

---

13 "Integrating Leadership Development and Business Performance," The Leadership Circle, accessed July 9, 2025, https://leadershipcircle.com/blog/reactive-leadership.

70–75% of top executives exhibit highly reactive behaviors: being critical, distant, arrogant, autocratic, overly driven, or overly passive and compliant.

This reactive orientation strongly correlates with leadership ineffectiveness and diminished business success, and it's simply a much less enjoyable way of living.

The road map for effective leadership involves maturing our reactive nature to higher-level expressions. This includes a caring connection with coworkers and colleagues, a mentoring relationship with those we lead, greater interpersonal intelligence, composure, community concern, and a higher vision and purpose beyond ourselves.

Greater self-awareness of how we impact others is perhaps the key to better business success. Leaders (spouses, parents) who understand that what matters is not only what they do but how they do it significantly outperform (in the most concrete sense) those who fail to grasp this.

The truth is that being an asshole is easy. It takes nothing to judge, criticize, or dismiss others. But this isn't leadership. It is assholeship.

Being a caring, self-aware, available, and gracious mentor, teacher, and coach to others is the real work of leadership. Of course, this requires maturity, patience, effort, and a commitment to our own personal growth. This work is hard. I know because I am forced to do it daily, and I can easily be an asshole.

We will either do our own inner work and excel, or we will soon find ourselves irrelevant to what the world needs and wants now: greater humanity.

Self-awareness is the ability to recognize how our thoughts and feelings shape our behavior and outcomes. It's the foundation of true business success and a deeply fulfilling life. We simply cannot effectively lead or influence others without first understanding ourselves.

What we are ultimately seeking through all this self-awareness—whether we realize it or not—is the ability to lead ourselves first. We want to be able to manage our emotions, choose our response, and act from intention rather than impulse.

What you are seeking is the ability to control yourself. Read that again. Because if you cannot control yourself, you will seek to control others.

This is how we fall into the *Outer Life Trap*: when we habitually focus on the outer world and use external events and people to define ourselves, confirm our success, and meet our needs for validation and love. Most of the time, we're unaware of our inner life and how central it is to everything we most care about.

When you fall into the Outer Life Trap, you may experience the following:

- You never feel as satisfied or fulfilled as you hoped or expected to at this stage in your life.

- You can be easily frustrated, judgmental, emotionally exhausted, and uninspired.
- You feel disconnected from yourself and others.
- You sense that you are missing out on your life because you lack the ability to enjoy the life, health, and success you have right now.
- You find it difficult, if not impossible, to be present. You are consumed with the past and/or future.
- You often want to be somewhere other than where you are. You always want or need more than what exists.
- You feel ineffective at work and with your family but haven't been able to take action so real change happens.
- You worry that life will never feel as you want it to and that you will never reach your full potential. You might ask, "Is this all there is?"

REFLECT: INNER LIFE LEADERSHIP ASSESSMENT: MY INNER LIFE CHECK-IN™

To better understand how you're currently experiencing your life, rate your initial reaction to each pair of phrases below. Each pair represents two ends of a spectrum.

How to complete:
For each item, choose a number from 1 to 5, where
- 1 = the statement on the left feels most true for you
- 5 = the statement on the right feels most true for you
Then add up your total score at the end.

1. I don't have a clear vision for my future. I don't feel excited today as I look ahead.	1	2	3	4	5	I have a clear, well-defined vision for my future. I feel excited today as I look ahead.
2. I'm unable to feel gratitude for my life as it exists.	1	2	3	4	5	I feel an abundance of gratitude for my life as it exists, even as I work toward creating a better future.
3. I'm concerned I will not ultimately live the life that I want or hope to live.	1	2	3	4	5	I'm living the life I want to live, or I'm confident that I will ultimately live the life I want and hope to live.
4. I don't feel I'm achieving my full potential. I feel stuck, confused, or lost. I'm not myself.	1	2	3	4	5	I'm living my potential each day. I love how I keep learning and growing. I like myself. Life feels fun.
5. I'm often bothered by my mind. I fight it daily. It's not enjoyable living within myself. I feel bad on the inside most days, despite my external success.	1	2	3	4	5	My mind champions and encourages me daily. I feel supported by my innermost thoughts. I'm grateful for all I have and am working toward. I love my life's journey.
6. I need outer indications of love and success to feel good. Others must be a certain way for me to be okay. I don't focus on developing a rich and rewarding inner life. I don't routinely work to foster the feelings I wish to feel. I expect them to come from people and situations outside of me.	1	2	3	4	5	I love and champion myself internally. I need little recognition or validation from others to enjoy my life. When outer validation comes, it's wonderful, but I don't need it. I generally feel great, regardless of what others say or do. I control how I feel, and I usually feel great.

7. I believe I'm neglecting and missing out on important elements of a meaningful life. Each day feels like a means to achieve some necessary end so that I can finally be enough, okay, happy, important, and successful.	1	2	3	4	5	I know I'm engaging and prioritizing the important elements of what I consider a meaningful life. I live each day as an end in and of itself. I'm not waiting on anything or anyone to enjoy my life. I'm enough as I am. I truly enjoy my life today.
8. I don't feel as much satisfaction, joy, and fulfillment as I desire. I find most experiences disappointing or lacking. I believe I need more (success, money, recognition, etc.) to feel the way I want to feel.	1	2	3	4	5	I feel as much satisfaction, joy, and fulfillment as I desire. There is so much beauty in everyday events. I have everything I need, and what I want comes easily at the right time. It's a marvelous unfolding that I trust completely.
9. I don't feel I have freedom in my life. I feel trapped to be a certain way and to do certain things. This doesn't feel like my life. I don't know how long I can keep this up.	1	2	3	4	5	I feel free. I know I create my own reality, and I'm intentional in what I create. I like knowing I'm the sole narrator of my life's journey. There are no ordinary moments. All of life is infused with richness. It's an honor to be alive.

	1	2	3	4	5	
10. I'm doubtful that focusing on my inner life will bring me what I seek. Most days, I feel bad on the inside, and I'm certain that I need things and people outside of me to change for me to feel okay.	1	2	3	4	5	I actively nurture a rich and rewarding inner life. I love that I'm getting better at being able to choose the thoughts I focus on, thereby controlling my entire experience of life. In most situations, I can find something beautiful to focus on and feel grateful for. I easily bring more presence, beauty, and joy to others.

Reflect:

- Why did I give myself that score?
- How do I feel about my scores?
- What one statement do I most want to improve?
- What one new thought could I choose to think that would improve that score?

Write it down and place it where you can read it daily (e.g., your bathroom mirror).

THE COST OF AN OUTER LIFE FOCUS

With our relentless pursuit of external success and fulfillment, a stark reality often goes unexamined: the profound cost of neglecting our inner life. This can lead to a pervasive sense of dissatisfaction, a feeling of never quite making it, no matter how many external milestones we achieve. It's a cycle where we perpetually defer our happiness and peace until the next achievement, the next accolade, which leaves us feeling empty and exhausted. It is sad that so many of my wildly successful clients don't feel successful.

The irony is palpable—we chase after a fulfilling life without realizing the key to such fulfillment lies not in external achievements but in nurturing the world within us.

For instance you might say to yourself, "When I achieve or have X, then I will be okay, successful, and happy," which sets you up for a conditional relationship with life, perpetuating an "If X, then Y" perspective.

You will then believe that you always need something external to feel the way you want and that could cause you to tell yourself: "I don't yet feel the way I hoped or wanted to feel, so I must still need more…money, admiration, people, or things."

This one thought, *If X, then Y,* could cause you to miss out on your entire beautiful life!

I have worked with countless clients who are endlessly frustrated: something or someone is always other than what they wish it or them to be. They fail to see that their way of thinking is causing them this constant frustration. They fail to see that we can never complain or beat ourselves up enough to create a great life. Because the way we live our inner lives directly influences our outer lives, if we want a great life experience, we need to decide to think great thoughts and know how to feel great feelings!

There is a better way: Cultivate a rich and rewarding inner life.

In chapter four, I will show you that Inner Life Leadership is about having an *Inner Life First Focus*, and you get that by:

- living today as you want and intend to live all your days;
- deciding how you will think about yourself, others, your life, and your work, and;
- learning to feel now the way you hope to feel in the future, without waiting to become, do, or achieve anything first.

The key is realizing that what you've been searching for begins with learning to cultivate the feelings themselves. This is the Inner Life Opportunity!

CHAPTER FOUR

THE INNER LIFE OPPORTUNITY!

There is a path to the life and leadership impact you're looking for, and it begins with a single decision: to choose where you will place your attention.

We've all had moments that instantly shift how we see the world. Imagine receiving a call from your doctor with devastating life-altering news. In that moment, everything else fades. Your priorities rearrange themselves in a heartbeat. But then, a second call comes in. There was a mistake. You're fine. Nothing is wrong.

Suddenly, the weight lifts. The sun seems brighter. You breathe deeper. You appreciate everything around you, all in the span of a few short minutes. Very little in your external world has changed, but everything feels different. That shift comes from inside you.

It's the same thing that happens when we fall in love. Life feels lighter, less urgent, more generous. We credit the other person;

but the truth is, it was always us. We changed how we thought, how we felt, and how we perceived the world.

You can focus on your outer life and hope your inner life keeps up. Or you can focus on your inner life—and watch everything else transform.

BIG IDEA #4: DEVELOP AN INNER LIFE FIRST FOCUS

This isn't about ignoring your goals, dreams, or ambitions. They matter deeply. It matters that you go after the life you imagine, that you chase what lights you up, and strive to achieve what you are not even sure you're capable of. You are meant to create, build, and expand.

But I'm inviting you to also, simultaneously, learn to foster the inner life experience you're truly seeking through those goals. Because if you don't learn how to feel the emotions you long for (e.g., peace, joy, freedom, aliveness, confidence) on the way to your dreams, you won't magically feel them when you get there. The larger house, big promotion, new relationships, or higher income will simply bring new challenges if you haven't developed the capacity to feel how you most want to feel right now.

You can start this work by directing more of your attention to all the beauty, joy, and success that exists in your life today. Doing so allows you to feel more fulfilled right now while becoming more attuned to the opportunities around you. From that place of gratitude and presence, even more becomes possible.

Life is far more precious and beautiful than we can possibly conceive. But to see it, we must pause the mental noise, the endless stories we tell ourselves, and simply observe.

Imagine savoring the everyday: drinking your morning coffee, greeting your family, acknowledging coworkers before a meeting. Feel the awe of nature, the pride in a job well done, the energy of a strong presentation, or the connection of a shared laugh. Notice your health, a kind word from a stranger, or your admiration for an artist's creativity.

When you truly see these moments, they deepen your connection to the present and everything that is already working well. The world is filled with so much beauty, but most of us haven't developed the eyes to see it.

PRACTICE #4: A DAILY MORNING PRACTICE

I've shared this idea with over 12 million people in the last few years alone, and it consistently connects and delivers real results.

Set aside five minutes every morning. Set a timer if it helps you.

- Write down an intention for the day.
  - » How do you want to handle the million and one things required of you? For example, you might say, "I want to be present to the people in my life today," or "I want to be approachable, encouraging, and inspiring with those I need to collaborate with today."
- With the remaining time, write down as many good, exciting, and inspiring thoughts as the day ahead could hold for you—*if you only let it.*

For example, I might write, "I want to feel excited and inspired today. To feel this way, I will need to remember that I once dreamt of writing my own book, and it is getting done, it is getting close to completion, and it will soon be out in the world to assist others. I am truly living a dream of mine!"

Whatever you do, please don't dismiss the Daily Morning Practice as too simplistic or overly optimistic. If you are diligent in this daily work, I promise your life and leadership impact will begin to unfold for you in ways you perhaps cannot yet conceive of.

Put in the work. Commit to this practice consistently for at least one month before evaluating its impact.

You'll soon discover that something so simple can truly transform your life. I've witnessed it in countless clients, from CEOs of multibillion-dollar organizations to teenagers navigating the storm of middle school.

You'll immediately become more present and effective with those you work and live with, because when you feel good, you will be good for others.

The sentence above might be the most important sentence in this entire book. Read it again.

The inner work I propose requires awareness, discipline, and effort upfront. But the more you focus on new, exciting, inspiring, and encouraging thoughts, the more those thoughts will strengthen new and different neural connections. Before you know it, you'll realize that your entire experience of yourself and the world has changed. We'll explore this idea more deeply soon, but for now, know this: Change your thinking, and you change your life.

The Payoff of Cultivating a Rich and Rewarding Inner Life

- Even in the midst of life's challenges, you'll experience spontaneous moments of joy and connection—with yourself and others.
- You'll genuinely like yourself, feeling more alive, free, loving, and present.
- People will appear more beautiful, and you'll find yourself more open and engaged with the world around you.
- Ordinary moments will feel filled with beauty, meaning, and purpose.
- You'll feel grounded and clear, living more intentionally and aligned with what truly matters to you.
- You'll accomplish more with less effort and stress, as opportunities begin to flow more naturally.
- You'll feel a deep sense of calm and contentment in the present, while still feeling energized and hopeful about what's ahead.

I saw a real-life example of the power of this inner work at the end of a coaching engagement, when one client noted that "There used to be a lot of jerks in my world. I don't know where they all went!"

This change came from taking a hard and somewhat painful look at how they saw themselves and others. "I didn't realize how negative I had become," they admitted. "My negative nature created adversarial expectations. I didn't realize how often I made myself feel wrong."

As they voiced their thoughts to me, they began to see how harshly they judged themselves. "No matter what I did, I told myself I should have done something else. I constantly felt I was failing despite being at the top of my field, so I viewed everything and everyone else in a negative light."

The turning point for each client came when they traced the voice of that inner critic back to its source. They said, "Once I realized I had this subtle, but ingrained, way of thinking, I stopped paying so much attention to that negative, critical voice, one I've come to learn came from my mother."

This client's journey of self-reflection revealed more about their upbringing. "My mom was strict and demanding, and I didn't realize for a long time how that shaped my impatience with myself and others. Now I try to treat everyone with respect. I know I can learn from anyone, and I'd rather support and mentor others than waste time criticizing or complaining."

Other clients have shared similar insights. One said, "I spent years trying to prove I mattered, trying to be someone important, someone people liked, admired, or listened to. Every interaction felt like a test of my worth. I just wanted to feel equal, like I belonged."

They continued, "What I've come to realize is I always did. I've always been someone. Now that I see that, I no longer need to chase validation. That's what real freedom feels like. I can simply show up fully, connect with people, and focus on what

I'm here to do, instead of carrying a chip on my shoulder about what I need to get in order to feel okay."

MORE INNER INTENTION

Tell me your thoughts, and I will tell you your future. We become what we think about. It can be no other way. That is not just a nice idea; it is neuroscience. The more we think a thought, the more likely we are to think it. And it is by repeating a thought that we strengthen particular neural pathways until they become automatic, well-worn paths our brains easily travel down without us even needing to be present for it. Repeated thoughts become familiar, and with that familiarity, we begin to accept the thoughts as truth. But repetition or familiarity doesn't make the thought any truer; it only makes it habitual.

Think of it like a social media algorithm. If you search "the world is flat," your feed will quickly become saturated with posts, videos, and content that reinforce that idea and others like it. Soon, it can feel like everyone believes it, and maybe you should too. Your brain works the same way. If you repeatedly think *I'm not good enough,* your mind will begin filtering and interpreting the world in ways that reinforce that belief. But if you redirect your attention to a new thought, like *I am here, and I can help others*, the same mechanism begins working in your favor.

This isn't about pretending everything is positive or ignoring hard truths. It is about becoming intentional with your mind, consciously choosing which thoughts serve you and other people and which do not. Lasting success, joy, and fulfillment are not accidents. They are the result of focused, deliberate thought. Without intention and training, the human mind tends toward the negative. Everything else requires intention and discipline.

Your present reality is simply a reflection of past thinking. It says little about what is possible if you begin thinking differently today. You are always one thought away from a new feeling, new decision, and new result. What you focus on expands. So what thoughts will you feed your mind?

REFLECT: CHOOSE THREE CORE THOUGHTS

In chapter three, I asked you to capture three thoughts you had this morning. I did this to have you bring more awareness to where you currently place your inner attention.

Now I want you to be intentional, to choose what thoughts you want and need to focus on. Write down three thoughts that are critical to you becoming the person and leader you intend to be. These should be thoughts you can return to daily, mental anchors that guide your actions, calm your mind, and reconnect you to your values.

Here are mine, thoughts I have practiced for years and that I believe have directly shaped my success:

- I can do anything I want to do; I only have to want to do it.
- I am disciplined and resourceful. I can always figure out a next step or ask for help.
- Integrity, service, and value will always be rewarded. Stay your course.

These thoughts were not just affirmations. They became instructions for how I moved through my day, how I overcame self-doubt, and how I created what I deeply desired.

Now it is your turn. Choose three thoughts that will serve as the foundation of your inner life, thoughts that remind you who you are and what you believe (or are going to need to believe) about yourself in order to be who and all that you are.

MORE INNER AWARENESS

How Do You Feel?

As I mentioned earlier in chapter three, many of us struggle to name how we feel. We are so busy living our lives and doing all that is required of us that we often don't take the time to check in with ourselves emotionally. For many, however, this isn't just about time; it's a developmental gap. Let me explain.

Society has long conditioned boys, for example, to disconnect from their emotions. They were often told to "stop crying or I'll give you something to cry about" or to man up when showing any sign of vulnerability. Today, when I ask my male clients how they feel, they often respond with what they think. When I ask again, they genuinely don't understand the question. Of course, not all men were raised this way, and some women were, but many people never had the chance to learn the emotional awareness that is now essential in leadership and life.

Yet we expect leaders of all kinds to be emotionally intelligent and self-aware. We ask them to inspire, connect, listen, coach, and regulate themselves under pressure, even though many were raised to ignore most of their feelings, aside from anger, which seemed to be more socially acceptable. Developing the ability to recognize how our thoughts make us feel and how our feelings result in our behavior is necessary work for all of us.

If we want to live our dream lives and have the impact we imagine, we must become fluent in our emotional world. We must ask: *How do I feel? How do I want to feel?* (Refer back to the Feelings Wheel in chapter three to help identify and articulate what's truly going on beneath the surface.)

It may seem obvious that tuning into your emotional experience is important, but it's surprisingly uncommon. Many of my clients, people who are objectively some of the most powerful, successful, and wealthy individuals in the world, do not often feel powerful, successful, or wealthy. They feel protective, behind, under pressure, or unseen. They compare themselves to others, focus on what is still missing, or are overwhelmed by the weight of their visibility and responsibility. We can all feel powerless at times, because we are, ultimately, only one person. Even if we do great work in the world, it can feel like it's not enough. As Gandhi said, "Whatever you do will be insignificant, but it is very important that you do it."

Far too many of us do not feel wealthy. Our abundance has become commonplace. Or, if we are aware of it, we live in fear of losing it, of still not having enough, or of being surpassed by others. This is why inner awareness matters so much. Without it, we miss the pretty great life we have right now.

Just like we practice identifying and choosing our thoughts, we must learn to identify and choose our feelings. A critical step toward making your tomorrow better than today is to decide how you want to feel and learn how to feel that way now. For example, if you want to feel confident, calm, successful, or joyful, you must practice feeling those emotions today.

Personally, I want to feel healthy, present, creative, innovative, and free. To feel this way, I must practice these emotions daily. For example, to feel healthy, I pay attention to how young and strong I am today. I know that in 20 years, I likely won't feel as physically capable as I do right now, and I would probably give anything to come back to this moment and appreciate the youth and mobility I have. That awareness helps me feel healthy now. It also gets my butt to the gym.

To feel free, I remember that as an entrepreneur, I can choose when and how I work. I joke that I get to work any 18 hours a day I like, but the truth is that I have more freedom than most people on the planet. I can easily forget this fact when I'm staring at an overwhelming to-do list, but it's true and important that I remember that truth. When I bring these thoughts into focus, I feel my own health and freedom daily.

Feelings are not simply passive. Some arise automatically, yet we can and must choose how we will feel. In case you haven't noticed, adult life and leadership tend to offer only problems. Unless you want to be frustrated and upset every single day, you must choose otherwise, which makes this choice even more essential.

REFLECT: FOSTER FIVE FEELINGS

Using the Feelings Wheel from chapter three to prompt you (but of course, don't limit yourself to only those listed), select five words that describe how you want to feel each day, how you most dream of feeling!

Write these five words down. Place them where you can see them each morning. Add reading them aloud to your Daily Morning Practice.

Let these words guide how you think, what you do, and how you show up. Because the way you feel consistently is the life you are living.

Again, I most want to feel healthy, present, creative, innovative and free. How do you most want to feel daily?

MORE INNER EXPLORATION

Let's continue our inner life exploration by becoming even more aware of what occurs within you. This will allow you to more intentionally choose how to respond in the external world. What you focus on internally, you create externally:

- Thoughts and feelings of lack lead to the experience of lack.
- Thoughts and feelings of frustration and problems create a life filled with frustrations and problems.
- Thoughts of exciting possibilities and solutions generate energy, innovation, solutions, and new opportunities.

You can choose to focus your thoughts on the problem of the day or the flaws of others. And many people do, though it is a very unrewarding way to live. If you're frequently disappointed, frustrated, or angry, this may be why.

This is the antithesis of leadership.

You can also choose to focus on past wounds or your perceived flaws. But doing so isn't just unhealthy; it's also self-absorbed. Focusing primarily on yourself causes you to interpret everything as being about you. If you're easily jealous, hurt, depressed, or offended, this may be why. I know because I spent years practicing this.

So let's explore how to become more aware of all that is happening within you, because it is most likely responsible for your entire experience of life!

Here's a simple but powerful formula:

Thoughts + Feelings → Behavior → Impact and Results

Let's explore this formula with some real-life examples. Consider the following:

Your CFO resigns. A merger proceeds. A key leader is let go. You lose a major deal. Your direct report mishandles an important task. A water pipe bursts in your home. Authorities warn of a new pandemic virus. Your children make choices you wish they hadn't. Your spouse uses a certain tone of voice. World leaders take actions that scare and affect us all.

How do you react?

Do you find yourself wanting to vent to anyone who will listen, perhaps instantly taking to social media? Do you look for someone or something to blame, righteous about the fact that this should not be occurring? Do you allow yourself to feel hurt, angry, scared, sad, or disappointed? Or do you mostly cover up your real emotions with a facade you believe to be more socially acceptable? Perhaps you shut off, go numb, and as Brené Brown put it, "have a couple of beers and a banana nut muffin."[14]

On the other hand, maybe you find yourself relaxed and able to easily lean into the event. Are you open, curious about the news and eager to research it fully, taking nothing at face value? Do you focus on any opportunity the event could bring? Perhaps you are quick to see the humor, and you use the event as material for your next comic routine.

Which reaction do you find yourself falling into or choosing most often?

BETWEEN STIMULUS AND RESPONSE

We might all react in any of the ways listed above. Sometimes, we are genuinely curious and can focus ourselves to improve or advance a situation. Other times, we quickly find the humor and use it to steady ourselves and others for a future we had not quite anticipated nor wanted. Then, there are those times when we are in shock: emotionally triggered, overwhelmed, and unable even to think, so we seek someone who will listen, all in an effort to make sense of what has occurred.

How we react depends on how we think of ourselves and the meaning we give an event: something occurs and instantly our

---

14 Brené Brown, "The Power of Vulnerability," talk delivered at [event if known], [location if known], [date if known], transcript, 16:51, Rev.com, https://www.rev. com/transcripts/brene-brown-the-power-of-vulnerability.

internal narrative—who we think we are (our self-identity) and how we believe events should unfold and people should behave—is activated.

Pay attention: This is our moment to awaken!

Between stimulus and response lies our greatest opportunity to advance our leadership. It is in this nano space of time that we can decide to attribute meaning in a way that can most effectively direct our own and others' attention and energy well.

There is a quote—one that has evolved over time and is often misattributed—that can be traced back to psychologist Rollo May's work on human freedom. The version most often shared reads, "Between stimulus and response there is a space. I will meet you there."[15]

Between stimulus and response is our one rare opportunity to see what we are otherwise blind to: the box we put ourselves and others in, our internal narrative and habitual meaning-making patterns.

If we study ourselves, which is the work of leadership development, we can observe our usual ways of thinking about ourselves, interpreting events, and our very predictable response.

---

15 Rollo May, "Freedom and Responsibility Re-Examined," in *Behavioral Science and Guidance: Proposals and Perspectives*, ed. Esther Lloyd-Jones and Esther M. Westervelt (New York: Bureau of Publications, Teachers College, Columbia University, 1963), 103; see also Quote Investigator, "Between Stimulus and Response There Is a Space," last modified February 18, 2018, https://quoteinvestigator. com/2018/02/18/response/.

Ask yourself:

- What just happened?
- What did I just say to myself about what happened?
- What did I tell myself about what this means for me? About me? About who I tell myself I am?
- Is this a meaning I often give to events—an old identity, one that perhaps is no longer useful?

What fear do you often (re)activate within yourself?

Knowing the answer to this question is important, but knowledge alone is insufficient. We must be able to intervene between stimulus and response if we are to lead with the executive maturity required. The ability to slow down and recognize the space between—our one moment to be conscious and intentionally choose how we think about ourselves, our role, and the event—can be some of the most important work we ever do.

So the question again is: When something happens, how do you typically respond?

Consider something relatively benign, like your spouse forgot it was garbage day, or you have been overcharged by your telecommunications company.

How do you respond? What happens within you? What do you think and feel, and then what actions do you take? What is the impact of this behavior? Are you as effective and gracious as you could be? Would like to be?

Now consider something more serious, an event with larger consequences. What recent event upset you so much that you were unable to handle yourself well?

- What happened?
- What thoughts first came to your mind?
- What story did you tell yourself about what this meant for you? About you?
- Notice if this is a familiar story (e.g., I always get screwed over).
- Based upon that story, how did you respond?
- What was the outcome?

Notice now, in hindsight, other ways you could have responded.

Consider someone you admire: How might they have interpreted the same event? How would a different interpretation have changed your story, your actions, and then the outcome? Simply become aware that there were other choices than the one you made.

Life rarely, if ever, concedes to our expectations. Sometimes the events of our lives are better than we expect, and sometimes they are worse, but they are almost always different from our expectations. Therefore, it would serve us well to learn more about ourselves and how we react to external events, because the more we know about ourselves, the more we can steady, focus, and direct ourselves. The more we steady, focus, and direct ourselves, the more effectively we can lead others.

One thing is certain: Senior-level leadership will magnify immature ways of reacting as surely as alcohol and money magnify personality. We can all be highly reactive. See if you can find the conscious space between an event and your response today.

INTRODUCING THE SELF-INQUIRY TOOL (SIT)

To support this, I've created the Self-Inquiry Tool or SIT. This tool is designed to help you cultivate deep self-awareness and develop a richer inner life. SIT encourages you to pause and reflect on the dynamics at play within you at any given moment.

This is essential because even the best of us often operate on autopilot, reacting to situations without much awareness of why we're responding the way we are, the impact we are creating, and how we limit our own opportunities or make extra work for ourselves by behaving poorly.

SIT invites us to stop, sit, and ask, "What is happening within me?" This simple question can illuminate the thoughts, feelings, and behaviors that shape our interactions and outcomes.

By slowing down, identifying the situation, acknowledging our thoughts, recognizing our feelings, predicting our behaviors, and considering their impact, SIT helps us make more conscious choices. It allows us to act in alignment with our highest values and long-term goals, instead of being driven by lesser, older habits or external pressures.

SIT deepens our self-awareness and shifts how we approach life's challenges. It gives us the ability to respond with clarity and intention, leading to outcomes that are more aligned with what truly matters.

APPLY THE IDEA: USE THE SIT TOOL

Bookmark the SIT model and use it to reflect on events that either go exceptionally well or terribly wrong. Through the lens of SIT, you can turn the events of your work and life into actionable insight.

Consider a recent event and walk through the SIT questions, recording your answers. Remember, translating thoughts into words is not just an exercise but a powerful mechanism for more inner awareness, understanding, and change.

Here is how I used SIT recently:

- What's the *situation?* A direct report failed to follow through on a task.
- What am I *thinking?* Why can't anyone do their job? Do I have to do everything myself? Why can't I find good people?
- What am I *feeling?* Angry, frustrated, resentful, self-righteous.
- Based on my thoughts, how am I likely to *behave?* Short, rude, dismissive.
- What are the likely short- and long-term *impacts* of this behavior? In the short term, I treat my team badly. In the long term, I diminish and lose good people and gain a reputation as a terrible boss.

SELF-INQUIRY TOOL (SIT)
What's happening within me?

INTERNAL TO ME

THOUGHTS

- What am I thinking?
- What assumptions am I making?
- What story am I telling myself?
- What meaning am I giving to this situation?

FEELINGS

- How am I feeling?
- Mad, sad, glad, afraid, disappointed
- Pit in stomach, tightness in my chest?

SITUATION

- What's going on?
- What are people saying and doing?
- What are the facts?
- What would a video recording show?

SHARED WITH THE WORLD

BEHAVIOR

- Based on my thoughts and feelings, how am I likely to behave?
- What am I likely to say or do?
- What will my body language communicate?

IMPACT

- What is likely to happen as a result of my behavior?
- How will my behavior build or break trust?
- What are the likely outcomes for the business and the people involved?

INNERLIFELEADERSHIP

—— SUSANNE BIRO INC. ——

In this case, SIT made me rethink the situation. The stimulus was my marketing lead failed to follow through on an important task. My immediate response was frustration, so I took the opportunity to pause. Maybe I didn't communicate with her as clearly as I thought, or maybe she doesn't have the knowledge, experience, and understanding I thought she had, and hiring her was my mistake. In my case, I still believed she was a highly competent professional, so I realized I might just need to more clearly communicate my expectations. I might also need to teach her parts of the job I thought she should know to do but doesn't seem to. In this case, I used the SIT tool to ensure I built a stronger, more candid relationship, which helped us both in the future.

Without intentional awareness, I naturally become impatient, rude, and dismissive of others. Using SIT reminds me to pause, ask myself about the values I want to exhibit and the outcome I want or need, and then align my own thoughts, feelings, and behavior accordingly.

Stopping and managing ourselves well before interacting with and impacting others isn't easy, even for me. I don't profess to do any of this well, but I'm aware that when I'm short-tempered and rude, it's because I am not managing myself well inside. I'm also working toward being the person and leader I aspire to be; it is true that I teach what I most need to learn. Just know that there is power in the pause!

CHAPTER FIVE

GREATER SELF-KNOWLEDGE

What if, right now, you're at a pivotal moment that could reshape how you see life and leadership?

Can you consider the possibility that you, with all your quirks, limitations, and failings, are enough as you are?

What if the people you lead are too?

What if the very notion that we need to change ourselves or others to be effective leaders is a misconception?

Often, the problem is our endless drive for self-improvement or the desire to change others. What if the real journey of leadership involves simple acceptance?

What if all it took to be a more effective leader *and* live an incredible life was to simply be yourself? And that being yourself was not only enough but actually everything?

BIG IDEA #5: YOUR *SELF* IS EVERYTHING

Your self—the most real, honest, and authentic version of you—is more valuable than anything you could ever own or hope to achieve. Anything else is just a fraction of who you are.

Can you allow yourself to be your self?

Can you even conceive of the idea that nothing about you needs to change? This is a hard one, isn't it? It is for me, as being simply myself often feels boring and regular and human. Many of us have held this unconscious belief and worked to build up a persona for so long that we no longer know who we are versus who we thought we should or had to be.

Jim Carrey's story brings this idea to life. Known around the world for his comedic genius and larger-than-life roles in films like *The Mask*, *Liar Liar*, *The Truman Show*, and *Eternal Sunshine of the Spotless Mind*, Carrey built a career—and a public identity—by becoming whoever a script required him to be. But after fully immersing himself in the role of the eccentric comedian Andy Kaufman for the film *Man on the Moon*, he emerged shaken. He later admitted that the experience blurred the lines between character and self so deeply that he no longer knew where Andy ended and he began. What startled him most was the realization that even "Jim Carrey" was a role, just a less intentional one.

"I just thought I was building something people would like," Carrey reflected.[16] In trying to be accepted, he had unconsciously crafted a version of himself to meet the world's expectations. And many of us do the same. We shape ourselves to succeed, to fit in, to be liked. Watch yourself and you will see how much of your behavior is to please or impress others. It is

---

16   TIFF Talks, "Jim Carrey on *Jim & Andy: The Great Beyond* | TIFF 2017," YouTube video, posted September 11, 2017, https://www.youtube.com/watch?v=LM-nrH1CN4oc; and Jim Carrey, interview by *Variety*, "Jim Carrey on Losing Himself in Andy Kaufman for 'Man on the Moon,'" *Variety*, September 11, 2017, video, https://variety.com/video/jim-carrey-jim-and-andy-kaufman.

subtle, often unconscious, but real. Over time, we mistake the persona for ourselves and forget what exists underneath it all.

If you have ever had the thought *I don't know how much longer I can keep this up*, then you are aware that there is a persona you are trying to maintain. Jim Carrey's journey is a powerful reminder of how easily we can become the roles we play—and how liberating it is to begin letting them go.

HUMAN RELATIONSHIPS: HOW WE LEARN ABOUT OURSELVES

Human relationships are at the heart of everything that gives life meaning. After all, what would life be without others to share it with? The things we care about most—falling in love, laughing with family and friends, traveling and experiencing the world, or building something great—all require other people. Nothing meaningful happens in isolation. It all depends on our ability to be with others, and ideally, to genuinely enjoy their presence. Other people make life worth living. And yet, many of us also feel, as the French writer Jean-Paul Sartre famously said, that "Hell is other people." When we don't know ourselves well, we can feel uneasy in the presence of others, especially when they don't meet our unspoken expectations.

To protect ourselves, we begin to control who we allow in and how they must behave in order for us to feel okay. But the more we try to control life and other people, the more isolated and empty we feel. We are each so easily hurt. We must learn to turn inward, to understand our own minds and emotions, so we can meet any situation, not with fear but with curiosity, openness, and ease. Can you be at ease in the presence of others? At any social event?

That is what we're truly after: the freedom to be okay in any situation, to be fully present to life and enjoy it.

At our core, we want to journey with others, to feel a sense of belonging and camaraderie along the way. It is what makes this beautiful and often difficult and deeply painful human experience bearable—and meaningful.

Human relationships are how we learn, grow, and develop. As babies, we mimic our caregivers. As teens, we copy and assert ourselves in relationships with peers and previous generations. As adults, we learn from the feedback we get from others and the results we obtain (or fail to obtain).

Sure, there's a lot we can do on our own. For example, we can attend a silent meditation retreat in the hope of personal growth and improvement. This might be helpful, but only if we can apply our greater self-awareness to change how we interact with others in the real world.

Likewise, we can read ten books on self-development, but it only takes one moment of tension with a challenging colleague or family member to reveal how little we've mastered ourselves!

The spiritual teacher Ram Dass[17] once said, "If you want to know whether or not you are enlightened, go and spend a week with your family." Indeed, we can read a book or attend a course or meditation retreat, but one minute with a close loved one can show us how hard it is to truly practice what we've learned.

---

17   Ram Dass. *Still Here: Embracing Aging, Changing, and Dying.* Riverhead Books, 2000.

Dr. Wayne Dyer, another renowned spiritual teacher, prolific author, and speaker, known for works such as *Your Erroneous Zones* and *The Power of Intention*, used to tell the story of how during fights at home with his teenage daughter, she would say, "I wish the world could see Mr. Spirituality now!" I find this a great relief because I, too, have family members who tell me to "save your coaching for your paying clients," or "it is interesting how you don't live what you teach." Ouch. So I am eating humble pie right along with you. We all have work to do! And it is okay, as long as we stay open to doing it.

PRACTICE #5: TWO CHALLENGING PEOPLE

Use the following questions to reflect on two people you currently find challenging—one in your personal life and one in your professional life:

- What makes these people especially difficult for you? What do they do that throws you off or keeps you from being your best?
- What do these individuals reveal about your values, boundaries, or what matters most to you?
- How do you wish you could handle yourself in interactions with them?
- How might someone you deeply admire handle themselves with these individuals?
- What is one piece of advice you'd give yourself before your next interaction with each of them? Write it down and take your own good counsel.

As you reflect, remember: Inner awareness means learning to stay grounded and true to yourself, no matter how others act. Often, the people we find most difficult are the very ones life uses to help us become more aware, self-regulated, and whole.

LEARNING THIS LESSON WITH BETH AT THE GE EVENT

In 2006, I flew to Spain to teach coaching to 50 senior sales leaders at GE. Before the session, I was told that the client sponsor, Beth (not her real name), didn't have a high opinion of me. Apparently, she had attended one of the very first coaching programs I had ever facilitated, years earlier in Seattle, and she hadn't been impressed.

Truthfully, I didn't blame her. I was new to facilitation and likely wasn't as skillful as I should have been. Still, hearing that someone doesn't respect you is never easy.

Years earlier, this kind of feedback would have shaken me. I would have bent over backward to win her approval. But I had grown since the early days of my career. I made a conscious decision not to organize myself around her opinion or the need to change it. Instead, I focused on the 50 leaders I came to serve, people I knew would benefit from what I could offer *today*.

On the morning of the event, Beth took my co-facilitator and me to meet the GE president. As she introduced my colleague, she physically stepped in front of me, cutting me off from the interaction. They shook hands and began talking. I stood there, waiting for an introduction—but it never came.

I remember thinking, *How odd…I'm standing right here, but it's as if I'm invisible.*

Previously, a moment like that would have triggered all my insecurities. I would have tried to insert myself, probably in a way that came across as insecure or reactive. But this time, I stayed grounded. I observed rather than reacted. I noticed how anxious Beth seemed around her boss, and I didn't take it personally.

Just as I was about to introduce myself, the president turned to me and said, "I'm so sorry, who are you?" I smiled and replied, "Good morning, I'm Susanne Biro." We had a warm exchange and connected authentically, something only possible because I hadn't collapsed into fear.

Beth looked flustered. She quickly ushered us into the ballroom to begin. I chose not to match her energy, not to take on her panic or let it define the moment.

After the session, which was a tremendous success, Beth pulled me aside. "I'm so sorry I didn't introduce you this morning," she said. "I just really needed today to go well."

I replied simply and sincerely, "No problem, Beth. We're good."

What I learned that day was that I didn't need Beth's validation and approval. I needed my own. Placing ownership with her would have allowed me to abdicate my own responsibility over my emotions. Once I released her from my work, I needed nothing from her *or anyone else.*

This is leadership. It is the ability to work exceptionally well with and through others, up, down, across, and both inside and outside your organization. And it will demand nothing less than your own self-acceptance and validation.

RECONNECT WITH YOUR SELF

Do you ever feel like you're not quite yourself, like you're behaving in ways that don't reflect who you really are?

When I first started out in business, I struggled to attend most networking conferences. Everyone seemed eager to sell something, and I hated who I became in those rooms—competitive, insecure, fearful. I realized I'd need to find another way to market and sell, because handing out business cards felt phony, and I'm a terrible actress. If you've ever noticed a similar disconnect within yourself, you've caught a glimpse of your true self.

A critical part of self-awareness is knowing who you are. I'm not talking about job titles or social roles. I mean your self: the most alive, connected, real version of you.

Being ourselves sounds simple, but it isn't. In fact, it's been said that being ourselves is the hardest thing in the world.

Many of us spend our lives trying to get back to that truest version of who we are, peeling away the expectations, fears, and conditioning that buried this self.

Because you're reading this, you're already on that path. You're choosing to learn more about your thoughts and feelings and recognizing that to be better for others, you must first be better for yourself, deep within.

You matter more than you may realize. Your presence and your actions impact the lives of other people. You can make or break another person's day. Regardless of your past, you have the power, today, to become the kind of person you needed all those years ago.

So, I invite you to *(re)connect* with your self—the person you were before life hurt, silenced, or diminished you.

For me, that version showed up most clearly when I was five years old. I was enthusiastic, curious, funny, and full of joy. I never met a stranger. I loved learning about people and their dreams. I believed anything was possible and delighted in making others smile. I believed in people and challenged them to believe in themselves too.

But somewhere around 13, I began trading pieces of that girl for the approval of others. I began prioritizing their opinions over my own. Slowly, I lost touch with her.

For decades now, I've been making my way back. While I still value the input of others, I've learned to trust my instincts and show up with the same bold spirit I had as a child.

Recently, while writing an email to a potential client, I caught myself editing out everything that felt too enthusiastic, phrases like, "I would absolutely love to work with you." I worried it sounded unprofessional or overly eager. But the truth is that I *was* excited. So I let that genuine interest come through and hit send.

Since then, more than a few clients have told me they chose to work with me not just because of my experience or credentials, but because I seemed like I truly wanted to work with them. It turns out that being yourself isn't just enough; it's often the very thing that sets you apart.

REFLECT: WHO YOU'VE ALWAYS BEEN

You were born whole. Even if you've felt disconnected from yourself, your truest qualities are still inside you. Over time, the world may have shaped you in ways that caused you to hide or forget parts of who you are.

But those parts are still there.

Take a moment now to reconnect with yourself. Choose three to five qualities that reflect who you've always been, even if they've been latent for a while. These are not traits you wish you had, but they're ones that feel true deep within yourself. Let these words be a guide back to yourself.

Adventurous	Authentic	Brave	Bright	Calm
Caring	Cheerful	Clear	Compassionate	Confident
Connected	Considerate	Creative	Curious	Devoted
Encouraging	Enthusiastic	Expressive	Faithful	Friendly
Fun-loving	Generous	Gentle	Gracious	Grateful
Happy	Helpful	Honest	Hopeful	Humble
Imaginative	Intelligent	Joyful	Kind	Light-hearted
Loving	Loyal	Open-hearted	Optimistic	Patient
Playful	Present	Respectful	Sensitive	Spirited
Talkative	Thoughtful	Trusting	Warm	Wise

It's one thing to know who you want to be and how you want to feel. It's another to consistently live that out, especially when life gets hard. That's where daily practices come in. If identity is shaped by intention, it is reinforced by repetition. The following disciplines help you embody your chosen identity every day.

DAILY DISCIPLINES: BEING THE PERSON YOU WANT TO BE

Mental health is no longer a personal issue; it's a business-critical investment. The pressures of leadership today demand more than just strategic acumen and business insights. They require physical and mental stamina, emotional resilience, and the ability to deal with constant change and stress.

If you're in a position of leadership and running on fumes, feeling isolated, and questioning whether you can keep up with your workload, you are in good company. Burnout, poor health, and relentless technological change take a steep toll, affecting your family, morale, employee engagement, and ultimately, the bottom line.

We operate best when we honor the habits that align with our values and support our well-being.

I call these Daily Disciplines: the five to seven things that you know you need to do to live up to your own standards for leadership and life. These are the things that, when you do them, make you feel amazing. They allow you to be at your best for others, regardless of what life, family, and business throw at you.

Take time now to identify the daily actions that are critical for you to be most effective for the people and work that matter most.

For example, for me to be myself—someone who is excited by life, positive, enthusiastic, curious, and funny—I need to take exceptional care of my body and mind. As such, my Daily Disciplines include the following:

- Getting seven to eight hours of sleep.
- Doing the Daily Morning Practice I offered earlier.
- Reserving time each morning to prepare myself mentally for my clients, work, and family commitments that day. I am best when I do this very early in the morning, while everyone in my home is still asleep.
- Meditating and learning (generally through silence, reading, and podcasts) in the early morning and during any breaks, travel, or downtime.
- Exercising for at least an hour (yoga, Pilates, weights, a hike, bike, or walk).
- Drinking four to six glasses of water throughout the day.
- Eating lean and clean (ideally foods with one ingredient) and eating to 80% satiety.
- Spending time in nature, walking my dogs, with my family.

On my best days, I do all of these. On my worst, none. The goal isn't perfection. It's knowing what makes a great day for me so I can be great with other people. When I don't live these, I am kind of an asshole to others, so the point of the list is that I know how to get back on track when I fall off.

Now that you've seen my example, identify your own.

REFLECT: WHAT ARE YOUR DAILY DISCIPLINES?

- What daily actions are needed for you to feel your best?
- What habits enable you to be really great with and for others?

Write them down, commit to them, and revisit them regularly. Prioritize your health and nurture your well-being, and you'll not only sustain yourself but thrive in working exceptionally well with and through others.

YOU DON'T NEED TO CHANGE WHO YOU ARE

Many people today want to be stronger, more effective leaders. They attend seminars, take courses, and devour the latest leadership books, hoping to become great. But leadership has nothing to do with you being great. It has everything to do with doing all you can to make others great.

Just like in parenting, this isn't about you. It's about your impact. You are an instrument to serve others' greatest success. But you can only do that if you remain yourself, the clearest, strongest version of you—someone who knows how to meet your own needs, so you can focus on serving others.

Consider a recently hired CFO at a Midwestern healthcare company who reached out to me to work with her. The CEO specifically appointed her to bring a stronger human presence to a private-equity situation. She had a mild and gentle demeanor, which the private-equity partners perceived as weak and timid, leading to her being dismissed and ignored.

She would describe private-equity meetings as stepping into a shark tank. "It's really cutthroat, and they're such arrogant assholes," she said. "I don't want to be like what I see there. I don't want to have to become a bitch to get them to listen to me." Although others, including her CEO, advised her to be more of a shark in the shark tank, we explored the kind of leader she wanted to be. Her answer: "Who I have always been—kind, warm, clear, loving."

"Great!" I said. "How can you keep the very best of you, your humanity and kindness, and still give your audience what they want to know: a top line of how their money is performing?" "Yes, that's right," she said. "I need to walk in, give them the numbers and insight they care about, and then open the room for discussion."

She took that into the next meeting. She didn't need to raise her voice, curse or try to be intimidating. She simply needed to trust herself and focus on what her audience most wanted to know. Within a few meetings, the sharks began to realize that what they initially perceived as timidity was, in truth, quiet competence.

Deciding to be authentically herself enabled her to introduce more humanity into these meetings and eventually improve the organization's culture from the top down. She expressed that giving herself permission to be herself brought a profound sense of fulfillment, because she was leading in a way that resonates fully with who she is, wants, and intends to be. She saw firsthand how, by doing so, she led the culture, instead of being overly influenced by the other strong personalities within it, and she created a more human and effective environment for all.

We can live and lead from fear, and most do, but leading and living from love—fierce love—always wins. But this has to start with granting ourselves the freedom to be ourselves. We then know how to champion and encourage others to do the same.

IDENTITY: WHO YOU THINK YOU ARE

The very best leaders are more than just visionary and strategic; they also understand themselves deeply.

They aren't defined by external forces; they have a vision, a clearly defined set of values and goals, and they're intimately aware of how their inner life shapes their outer one.

This deep self-knowledge frees them from being tethered to a fixed past, granting them the flexibility to evolve into a person of their choosing.

Let's continue to build upon the foundational work you have done and explore something core to our behavior: our self-identity.

So who do you think you are? I don't think there's a more important question.

Look at the photo[18] below. Do you identify more with the person on the left or the person on the right?

Two men, worlds apart yet sharing the same street—a reminder that our self-perception shapes what we see and who we believe ourselves to be.

For years, I would have answered the guy on the right. Why? Because I often felt disheveled, not sufficiently put together, and always second or less than others—a bit of a loser, compared to the guy on the left who seems so confident, clean, and well put together.

---

18   Benjamin Disinger, *Hungry Homeless Man Sits Behind Wealthy Young Man*, 2020, photograph, Unsplash, https://unsplash.com/photos/man-in-black-jacket-and-black-pants-carrying-black-and-white-backpack-walking-on-sidewalk-during-2xzEIQFzw0g.

If you ask me now, I would still answer the guy on the right, but this time, for an entirely different reason. I identify as an artist whose sole purpose is to direct human emotion in a positive and useful direction. I am creative, resourceful, approachable, relatable, and finally comfortable in my own skin, needing little acknowledgment or validation from the outside world.

Take a few minutes and think about the person you most identify with in the photo.

- Why did you choose this person?
- What is it about them that resonates with you?
- How do you see yourself reflected by this image? Are you identifying with what you see as negative traits? Positive ones? Why?
- Ask yourself, "Is this how I want to perceive myself? Will doing so serve my goals, my family, and the work I feel called to do? If not, what self-identity will serve me better?

How we perceive the world is deeply intertwined with how we perceive ourselves. Our beliefs, values, and experiences act as lenses, coloring our interpretation of events and interactions.

Imagine two people witnessing a rainstorm. One, a farmer, sees much-needed nourishment for crops, while the other, a city dweller, sees a cause for traffic delays. This shows how our identities can lead to vastly different interpretations of the same event.

Our identity influences not only how we see the world but also the opportunities and choices we believe are available to us. In many ways, we each wear different glasses that offer us a unique view of reality, with only certain paths and choices illuminated. For example, someone who identifies strongly as a realist might dismiss their potential for creative or imaginative endeavors, not realizing the latent talents lying dormant within them.

Our identities are shaped by myriad factors, including family, society, ethnicity, and personal experiences. For instance, a child raised in a multicultural environment may develop a more inclusive and diverse worldview.

REWIRING YOUR BRAIN

In the grand narrative of our lives, the most profound superpower we possess is the ability to choose who we will be. This power, often underestimated, is the key to sculpting our identity, shaping our destiny, and living a life of our own choosing. As such, we must move from reacting to the world around us to proactively creating the world within us.

Think about the parable of the bricklayers. Often attributed to accounts about the building of St. Paul's Cathedral in London, the parable tells the story of a traveler who came upon three men working. When asked what they were doing, the first bricklayer replied, "I'm laying bricks, just as I have been told." The second one said, "I'm raising a wall to make a living and feed my family." The third one declared, "I'm building a cathedral!" It's a story often shared in leadership and motivational settings. But it's a popular story for a reason: It clearly illustrates the vital role we play in defining ourselves.

Are you a bricklayer? Are you working to feed your family? Or are you building a cathedral? Neither supersedes the others; each plays a vital role in our society. But the value of each role isn't what's important here. What's truly important is that we understand that by choosing our self-identity, we take control of our narrative, steering our lives toward the future we seek and intend.

As I shared at the start of this book, you don't have to be who you were yesterday.

As you may know, the scientific community used to believe our brains were set by age 30. However, we now know our neurons grow and recede according to use throughout our lives. So the more we think a thought, the more we will think it, and by repeating a thought, we strengthen a neural connection and shape the physical structure of our brains.

"By choosing which aspect of an experience to focus on, we can change the physical structure of our brains." Dr. Jeffrey M. Schwartz, a leading psychiatrist, neuroscientist, and researcher known for his work on obsessive-compulsive disorder (OCD) and neuroplasticity, explains this in his book *The Mind and The Brain: Neuroplasticity and The Power of Mental Force*[19].

Neuroplasticity, the brain's ability to form and reorganize synaptic connections, especially in response to learning, experience, or injury, means that every thought we choose can physically reshape our brain's structure. So by choosing what

---

19   Jeffrey M. Schwartz and Sharon Begley, *The Mind and the Brain: Neuroplasticity and the Power of Mental Force* (Harper Collins, 2003).

we think, we end up altering our perception of ourselves and our entire understanding of the world.

This scientific insight underscores the immense power of thought in redefining our identity and enabling us to break free from the shackles of past limitations.

In my practice, the first step with every client is to help them recognize their current thought patterns and who they believe they are. From there, we envision who they want to become and identify the core thoughts necessary to support that transformation. Embracing the concept of neuroplasticity, we work on altering these thought patterns. By consistently repeating new, empowering thoughts, my clients effectively rewire their brains, fostering new neural pathways that support their desired self.

One client's journey underscores this process. Their inner voice was harsh and critical, and he would say things like, "I'm such an idiot—do you still want to work with me?" This language of self-reproach was a barrier to progress. I encouraged him to stop using the language of his past. As someone who once downplayed myself at every turn, I understood the necessity of halting this negative self-talk. One of the most profound things we must overcome is how poorly we speak to ourselves. Even successful people fall into this pattern; it's one of the things that made them so successful. They demand a lot of themselves. This kind of talk fuels their drive. However, we can never beat ourselves up enough to create a peaceful life.

A negative inner monologue can easily seep into conversations with coworkers, friends, and family. Say "I'm so stupid" often enough, and people just might believe you. Worse, it can sap our joy and make us feel bad every day as we think "I should have done that better" or "I failed again." Then, of course, we start calling others stupid, too.

One of the tools I use often with clients is *Three Stories*. Essentially, I'll ask them to tell me a couple of stories to give me insight into the different chapters of their lives.

- "What was it like for you to be a small child?"
- "What's your 'coming of age' story from your early twenties?"
- "What's life like for you now; what chapter are you currently living in?"

These stories give my client significant insight into why they're encountering so many roadblocks in their path.

As one client reflected on his childhood, the source of his self-critical inner voice became clear: his father. Growing up, the only time his dad spoke to him was to reprimand him. He never heard the words he most longed for, like "You're doing great" or "I'm proud of you." Like many of us, he internalized that silence and criticism, carrying forward a belief that he was never manly enough, smart enough, or simply enough.

In his leadership role, this showed up as an almost constant inner pressure: *You should be doing more. You should already know this. You're falling short. Don't mess this up.* He unknowingly sought validation from his CEO and board, hoping their praise would finally quiet that inner voice. But no external recognition can ever fill the gap.

Once he saw the connection between his past and his present patterns, he realized he no longer had to live by those inherited words. He stopped repeating the language of his father and began building a new inner narrative, replacing the old voice with what he most needed to hear: *You handled that well. I'm proud of you. This is an impossible turnaround, and you are navigating it well.* Over time, these became not just words but how he began to experience life. And then how he coached and communicated with his senior leadership team.

It's imperative that we replace our inner critic with the words of an inner champion. We need ourselves on our own side if we are to succeed in all the ways we most mean that word, perhaps now more than ever.

YOUR CURRENT SELF-IDENTITY

Take a few minutes to consider who you've told yourself you are in this chapter of your life.

Without overthinking it, write down who you currently believe yourself to be.

For example, I currently think of myself as a wonderful mother raising two children. I also think of myself as a successful entrepreneur, an executive coach who helps CEOs and executives become more effective by knowing themselves more fully, which allows themselves to be more of who and all they are.

I also believe, deep within myself, I can serve and advance so many more people than I currently do. But up until now, I have been unable to scale my work and have my message, insights, and tools reach the masses.

This feels accurate to who I am as I write this, not knowing if anyone will read or benefit from this book. Yet, I am devoting hours and years to writing it because some part of me knows I have an important role to play in ensuring our future world has more love, grace, and humanity. I feel called to do more, so I am listening to that call. The result is this book and my podcast, *Deep Fear to Empowered Leadership in Business and Life* (www. DeepFearPodcast.com).

Who are you today?

Who have you told yourself you are?

LEARN FROM ADMIRATION

In chapter two, I asked you to think of someone you admire who has achieved the one personal goal you identified for yourself this year. I asked you to think about how they are living their life now and what they are likely thinking. Now let's build on that reflection.

A useful way to shape your chosen self-identity is by reflecting on the qualities you admire in others. Don't get me wrong; I'm not telling you to copy someone else's life. You're not trying to be someone else; you're trying to figure out who you want to be. The traits you admire in others often reflect your deepest aspirations.

Whom do you admire?

Think of people who inspire you (near and far, alive and dead) and list the qualities you admire in them. Be specific about the traits you admire most, such as:

Visionary	Disciplined	Honest
Courageous	Powerful	Resilient
Generous	Kind	Warm
Relatable	Fun	Funny
Witty	Smart	Skilled
Competent	Respected	Innovative

Reflect on why these traits resonate with you and what they tell you about yourself, about who you are, and who you must be in order for you to feel like yourself.

The person I admire most is my sister, Sharon.

Sharon is love personified. In high school, when she was in grade 12 and I was in grade 9, she would look for me at lunch to make sure I had something to eat. If I didn't, she'd give me her lunch. What teenager does that? She would also invite me to hang out with her friends, which instantly made me cool in the eyes of mine.

At the start of every school year, teachers would take attendance and ask, "Susie Biro, are you related to Sharon?" I'd smile and say, "I sure am!" Without fail, they'd respond, "We absolutely love Sharon. We are so excited to have you here."

She paved the way for almost everything good in my life.

Sharon has an extraordinary way with people, one that goes far beyond charm or social ease. It's her genuine presence, her attentiveness, and her unwavering belief that everyone she meets deserves to be seen and known. I've learned so much from her simply by watching the way she moves through the world.

Decades ago, we worked together in our mother's barbershop. While I focused on tasks, she focused on people. Her appointment book was always full, months in advance. Clients weren't just returning for a haircut; they were coming back for *her*.

She remembered names, life stories, and small details that most of us would overlook. Dave would walk in for his trim, and she'd greet him with, "I just saw your brother yesterday and asked how you and your mom are doing; now you can tell me yourself!" Jenny would stop by for a color, and my sister would say, "Last week, I saw the perfect dress for your daughter's recital and set it aside for you." She connected dots that made people feel valued—not as clients but as human beings.

That same gift of noticing, caring, and making others feel like they matter has followed her into her next chapter. Now as a home designer and small renovation project manager, she helps people create living spaces that are both deeply functional and beautiful beyond their dreams, all within the realities of their budget. And again, her work is in constant demand. She doesn't even have a website! People line up to work with her—not only because of her impeccable taste and creativity but because of the experience of working *with* her. She listens. She sees people. She makes the experience of creating their dreams fun and enjoyable.

Our mother used to say, "Do everything with love." My sister lives that truth. I tend to be more task driven. I've had to train myself to slow down, to first connect, to bring warmth and humanity into my efficiency.

I know I'll never be my sister. And that's okay—I don't want to be her. But I do want to grow more into the kind of person she naturally is: aware, compassionate, loving, kind, and in demand, not because of what she can do but more so because of how she makes others feel.

I do believe that love is the most powerful force on the planet. I often wonder why so many leaders fail to use it. I know that learning to "do it with more love" is responsible for every success I have today.

APPLY THE IDEA: CHOOSE YOUR IDENTITY—THE ULTIMATE ACT OF LEADERSHIP

In a world where so much is outside our control, one freedom always remains—our ability to choose who we will be. This is not simply about personality or temperament, and it is not claiming you are a cat when you aren't, but it is about consciously deciding to become a person worthy of your own genuine respect.

This is leadership at its most personal. It is the inner vision we hold for our own life. And like any vision worth realizing, it requires daily alignment, intention, and action.

Step 1: Define Who You Want to Be

Ask yourself: *Who do I most want to be in this life?* Not what others expect, not what you've been so far—but the clearest, boldest, most honest expression of who you feel you are and all you feel called to become. Write it down. Name it. Own it. This is your north star.

Step 2: Begin Each Day With Intention
Every morning as you do the Daily Morning Practice, reconnect with this identity. Write a sentence: *Today, I want to be...* Add words that reflect your intention, like "focused, clear, fun." Then, spend a few minutes writing thoughts that energize you about the day ahead. This primes your mind to live from your vision rather than old habits.

Step 3: Shape Your Inner Dialogue
We become the stories we tell ourselves. Be aware of your inner voice. When it speaks in fear, judgment, or defeat, gently redirect it. Replace "I'm failing" with "I'm learning." Replace "I am overwhelmed" with "I am learning how to handle the demands of this next level." Speak to yourself, as psychologist Jordan Peterson teaches, like someone you are responsible for helping, because you are.[20]

Step 4: Visualize the Life You Want
Close your eyes. Spend some time each week seeing yourself being the person you aspire to be. Where are you? What are you doing? How do you feel? Visualization is not wishful thinking; it is active and necessary mental training. Your brain doesn't distinguish vividly imagined experiences from real life. The more clearly you see what you want and intend, the more it occurs to you to take the actions that make it a reality.

---

20   Peterson, Jordan B. *12 Rules for Life: An Antidote to Chaos*. Toronto: Random House Canada, 2018.

Step 5: Live Your Daily Disciplines

You identified the five to seven actions that ensure you can be at your best for others. Review them. Are they still aligned with who you want to be? Adjust if needed.

This work may feel awkward at first. That's normal. You are choosing to lead your life from the inside out. And that is the truest freedom there is. Nothing in these five steps is likely new. But this book isn't about new information—it's about timeless truths that you must apply if you want your tomorrow to be better than today.

WHAT'S POSSIBLE NOW?

As a leader (or parent), you know that just because you can do something does not mean you should. It may feel quicker or easier to answer that question, respond to emails, or solve problems yourself, but every time you do what others or technology could do, you distract yourself from the work only you can do. You also limit others from growing and leading at their level (where we are heading in the next chapter!).

This is where it's easy to miss the mark. The real job of a doctor is not only to heal the patient physically but also to care for them emotionally, ensuring they feel safe, understood, and not alone. When this does not happen, the fear of a scary diagnosis can stress a patient and cause significant harm that undermines physical healing. The real job of a parent is not only to provide for and guide their children but also to be a steady, loving presence so they grow up feeling loved, secure, seen, and valued. When a parent's eyes do not light up when their child enters the room, those children often grow into adults who spend their lives searching for the love and validation that should have come from their parents. And the real job of a leader is not only to deliver results but also to attend to the emotional climate, developing people, shaping culture, and inspiring trust.

Some leaders like to say they are not emotional, only logical and rational. But neuroscience has made it clear that this is impossible. Antonio Damasio's research, highlighted in *Descartes' Error*, demonstrates that without engaging the emotional centers of the brain, humans are literally unable to make decisions.[21] Every choice, from the simplest to the most complex, requires emotional input.

We also know this from watching our own behavior. Rarely do we make purely logical decisions. We almost always make emotional ones and then use logic to justify them, even if only to ourselves. Think about your own buying habits or how you choose to spend your leisure time, and you will see this truth.

Attending to emotions, our own and others', is not secondary work. It is a critical aspect of our life and work.

Throughout this book, you've gained insights to help you focus and see things differently. Now, take a quick self-survey to help you navigate a future where rapid change is the only certainty.

---

21 Damasio, Antonio R. *Descartes' Error: Emotion, Reason, and the Human Brain.* New York: G. P. Putnam's Sons, 1994.

Write down your answers to these questions:

1. What is my real job?

- What is it that I really do; what are the tangible and intangible results I am tasked with delivering?
- What is the value only I can bring?
- At my level, what are the two or three priorities that deserve most of my focus?
- Where are my presence and attention needed and irreplaceable?
- What decisions and communication must come directly from me to carry weight?

2. How am I spending my time now?

- Where do I currently invest my time and energy?
- Does this align with what matters most?
- What needs to shift in how I allocate my attention, focus, and time?

3. What must I let go of so others can grow?

- Which responsibilities should be owned by others?
- Who on my team can step up, or who must I develop to take on those responsibilities?
- What tasks could and should be automated or streamlined with technology?
- What investments in people or technology must I make now to prepare for the future?

As you reflect on your real job, what do you need to stop doing and what do you need to start?

Leadership is never lived in isolation, which is why once you've chosen who you want to be as a leader, the real test comes in how you show up with others—which is where we're headed next.

CHAPTER SIX

INTERACTING WITH OTHERS

E very true act of leadership has one purpose: to make life better in some meaningful way.

At its core then, leadership is rooted in our humanity. Yet far too often, we hide behind a professional mask of who we think we should be, only to lose connection with ourselves and the people we are meant to serve. When we approach roles of leadership as tasks to complete rather than relationships to honor, we generally miss the mark entirely.

It's like going to a doctor during one of the most vulnerable moments in your life, when you're in pain, scared, or waiting on life-changing news, and being met with a cold, detached demeanor. No warmth. No sense that your fear, loss, or confusion matters. In that moment, you may receive the correct diagnosis and the proper treatment plan, but you leave feeling worse: invisible, dismissed, and profoundly alone.

Contrast that with a doctor who sits down beside you, looks you in the eye, and gently says, "I know this is hard. I'm here with you, and we'll take it one step at a time." Same diagnosis, same treatment plan, but an entirely different experience. One leaves you shaken. The other leaves you feeling safe and supported. The interactions you have as a leader and the way you approach them can have the same vast impact.

That's the difference humanity makes.

But being human is hard—perhaps the hardest thing we'll ever do. Many of us pursue leadership roles in search of power, control, and authority. Yet to be human is to be vulnerable, fallible, and limited in control, capacity, and understanding— traits we often resist our entire lives. (It's no wonder we love superheroes; they offer a temporary escape from the limitations of our human form.)

We rarely grasp the power of our own humanity until life brings us to our knees, through difficult feedback, missed promotions or opportunities, job loss, divorce, aging, illness, or death. Humble pie, it turns out, is beneficial for most of us.

WHEN YOU LEAD WITH HUMANITY

Let me tell you a story.

Monica, a senior leader at a global tech company, was known for her sharp mind and high standards. She delivered results, met impossible deadlines, and expected the same from everyone around her. But recently, in a 360-degree feedback process, she received input that forced her to rethink her actions. Her team often felt intimidated, afraid to bring her bad news, hesitant to share bold ideas, and in some cases, were going around her entirely to get their voices heard.

Monica had grown up in a household where success was the only language spoken. Her father often praised her older siblings with phrases like, "That's how you make the family proud," or "We love seeing winners in this house." Although the words were never stated explicitly, Monica learned early that affection and attention followed achievement.

By the time she reached adulthood, Monica had perfected her ability to perform, excel, and lead with precision. But she had also internalized the belief that to be respected, she had to always be in control, never show uncertainty, and always have the right answer.

Through our work, Monica began to gently examine and challenge these beliefs. Slowly, she started opening up to her team. She shared stories of past mistakes, the anxiety she still felt before major presentations, and how imposter syndrome followed her even after years of success. As she became more honest, her team began to relax. Meetings became more open and energetic. People brought forward creative ideas, challenged each other respectfully, and took ownership of decisions without always defaulting to Monica.

For the first time in her career, Monica felt connected. She no longer had to project a mask of perfection or be the sole engine of excellence. She felt something new and deeply satisfying: colleagueship and camaraderie. And with it, she finally understood what authenticity in leadership really meant and what it would demand of her.

For Monica, being willing to be a mere mortal alongside the rest of us revealed itself not as weakness but as the very source of her strength.

WHEN YOU ACCEPT YOURSELF, OTHERS CAN TOO

To lead with humanity, we must first accept our own.

James, an executive vice-president and the single father of two teens, used to believe he had to be the strong, steady parent. But this left his kids feeling like they could not talk to him when they were struggling. After a difficult year for the family involving a separation, move, new school, and divorce, James finally opened up. He shared how hard things had been for him, too, how much he wished things had been different and how bad he felt. His vulnerability created space for honest conversation. Instead of feeling alone, his kids felt connected to their dad as someone who could relate to their pain, confusion, and loss. James learned that sharing what was real was healing for them all. He could listen without fixing, and in the process, he realized that the connection they all most yearned for existed here, too, in the loss and pain.

And then there's me.

In my master's program, I received feedback that I couldn't make sense of at the time. People called me stoic. I didn't even know what that word meant. In group work, classmates said they couldn't connect with me. One person told me I had no empathy, that I was all task and no emotion. Others said I came across as a know-it-all and that I was arrogant. A professor once asked me to stop interrupting and let her try to teach me something. At the time, I was confused and defensive. I thought it was important to project confidence, that I had it all together. But inside, I couldn't understand why I felt sad, exhausted, and deeply lonely. I was trying so hard to get it all right.

It wasn't until I was pushed, really pushed, to connect that something finally cracked open. I broke down crying in class one day, overwhelmed by the pressure of always being the strong one, the one who didn't need anything, the one who could perform and carry on without burdening others. It came from childhood. My parents had focused so much on my older sister, who had nearly died as an infant, that I learned to be the easy child, the one who didn't add any more weight to an already heavy load. I didn't know how I felt because no one ever asked me. However, no one ever asked me because I always looked like I was doing great. I campaigned hard for that image, always showing up polished and self-sufficient. Many of us who identify as strong or responsible know what it's like to over-function, hide our needs, and then wonder why no one ever checks in on us.

As I cried, one classmate said, "We want more of this side of you."

"What? You want me to break down crying? You guys are so weird," I said, half joking.

I didn't know how to strike the balance between keeping a protective wall up and letting it all fall. For a long time, I lived between that binary. It took me two full years to discover that there was a third way. I learned that I could connect without losing myself, that boundaries and authenticity are not opposites. In fact, it was only by respecting my boundaries and accepting all of me—my history, my limits, my strengths, even my awkwardness—that I found this other way.

Even now, as a deeply introverted person, I can be socially awkward. I sometimes say the most ridiculous things when all I'm trying to do is connect. If you meet me in a room where I don't have a clear role as the facilitator or the speaker, you might see that side of me. When attending social functions, I tend to find an extrovert and stay close to them as their ease makes the room feel safe for me.

But here's the difference: Now I meet myself with compassion. I accept that I do get nervous and sometimes overly enthusiastic in certain social situations. I'm basically a golden retriever in human form. And rather than hide that, I now find it funny. My husband and I will laugh at how I will meet someone and immediately invite them for dinner because I don't seem to be able to regulate my enthusiasm! Or, if we are about to meet new people, he will say, "Hey, don't screw this one up by being all weird, okay?"

Accepting myself the way I authentically am has changed how I connect with others. If we want to form real connections, we must begin by offering more compassion and humanity to ourselves, first inward and then naturally outward.

One of the most immediate ways our inner state influences the outer world is through the words we choose.

LANGUAGE MATTERS

Language matters more than we realize. It is not just how we communicate; language is how we experience the world. Every word we choose, the tone we take, and the way we express our thoughts becomes what we experience: "That meal was amazing!" versus "The food was okay."

In leadership, the language we use can uplift or undermine, include or isolate. Most of us were taught some version of the old phrase "Sticks and stones may break my bones, but words will never hurt me." It is a comforting idea, but it simply is not true.

Words can hurt, and words can heal. They can seal an important business agreement or lose a critical sale. They can sustain a relationship or end it. Words can create grace, understanding, and acceptance in the face of grave mistakes, or they can initiate legal battles and start wars. The language we use matters deeply, and it is our job to be thoughtful and intentional in how we use it.

We are all responsible for guiding the attention, energy, and talents of others—whether at work or at home. The language we use shapes how others experience a situation. Words influence culture, possibility, and performance. They are, without question, one of our most powerful tools.

For example, here are two ways to describe the same person:

1. Savio is thoughtful and thorough. He double checks his data and always raises potential risks early. He's the kind of person who prevents problems before they happen.

2. Savio is overly cautious. He slows things down by second guessing every decision and always finds something to nitpick. It's hard to get anything across the finish line with him.

I am not suggesting one is more honest than the other. The second description might be more accurate. But which one makes you trust Savio more with a complex project? And which one makes you want to exclude him from fast-moving initiatives?

Now consider if you used one of these descriptions in a conversation with a colleague, which would reflect better on you? How would it influence how they view your character, judgment, and leadership? Just by listening to you, people can tell instantly whether you're thinking at the right level for your role or the role to which you aspire. When you speak poorly of others, it shows poorly on you. Read that again. If Savio is truly ineffective, as his boss, you should have a conversation with him so that he becomes aware that he often holds projects up unnecessarily.

The words we use when speaking about people or situations are just as important as the ones we use when speaking to them.

Language reveals how we think. It gives others an often unintended glimpse into our inner life. We reveal our level of personal development by what we choose to focus on and how we express it.

For example, my husband has repeatedly pointed out that I tend to use absolutes like *always* and *never*. He shares that it feels exaggerated and makes him stop listening. A business colleague later echoed the same observation, noting that it diminished my credibility and made my point sound like hyperbole.

A more personal example for me is how I've chosen to speak to my children, especially now that they're teenagers. I've always talked to them the way I want to be spoken to: with respect, calmness, and honesty, even when I'm disappointed or frustrated. I treat them the way I want to be treated, and it has shaped the way we relate to each other.

Take something simple, like unloading the dishwasher. When they forget, I don't raise my voice or shame them. I'll say, "Hey, I'm disappointed. We all have things to do, and when you don't follow through, it creates more work for the rest of us." Almost always, they respond with "I'm so sorry, Mom," and they go do it right away—not because they're afraid of getting in trouble, but because they understand the impact of their actions.

And it works both ways. When I forget something they've asked of me, like signing a permission slip they need for school, I get the same treatment. They'll say, "Mom, I really needed that signed," and I'll respond with the same sincerity they've shown me: "You're right, I'm so sorry. I'll do it right now."

This mutual accountability didn't just happen. It was built on years of speaking to one another with respect. We hold each other to our promises, and we apologize when we miss the mark.

It's not perfect, of course. But it's real, and it's respectful. And it's exactly the kind of relationship I want to have with the people I love most.

Consider a boss who misses a long-standing one-on-one meeting with a team member. The employee had prepared carefully and was looking forward to discussing their growth. The next day, the leader sends a message that says "Something came up."

Technically, it may be true. But messages like that fall flat. They fail to acknowledge the impact of the missed meeting on the person at the receiving end. When communication is reduced to vague, impersonal phrases, we risk creating a culture where people feel like afterthoughts rather than valued contributors. This is how workplaces drift into environments where individuals become resources.

People respond to human language, not corporate jargon. A sincere message such as "I'm sorry I need to reschedule our meeting. Your time and goals matter. How does 3:00 p.m. on Friday sound?" does so much. It communicates respect, care, and responsibility. In an increasingly automated world, your ability to speak with heart may be your greatest competitive advantage.

HOW WE USE AIRTIME; IT MATTERS

What someone says reveals exactly where they allocate their most valuable resource: their inner attention. Pay attention. Start by observing others: What do they choose to talk about in their limited time with you? Are they thoughtful, gracious, and generous in their language or cold, negative, or disrespectful? What words do they routinely use? Which are helpful? Which might be limiting or harmful?

Now flip the lens: Ask yourself the same questions. What do you choose to discuss in your limited time with others? What words do you routinely use, and which ones improve your family, your team, and your business? Which might hinder or harm? What tone of voice do you typically use? What's your default tone under pressure?

Recently, I attended a business event where this truth was on full display. A CEO of a pharmaceutical company was invited to speak in a facilitated conversation with a woman whose husband had died shortly after being prescribed one of the company's drugs. They had agreed in advance to demonstrate what it looks like to have courageous, difficult conversations from opposing and emotionally charged perspectives.

The widow went first. She spoke with visible pain and raw honesty about losing her best friend and the father of her children, a healthy man in his forties who collapsed and died not long after starting the medication. Her voice trembled. She was grieving, furious, and desperate for an answer.

Then the facilitator turned to the CEO. This was his moment to lead with humanity—not to admit legal blame, but simply to say what needed to be said: "I am so very sorry for the loss of your husband and your children's father." But he didn't say it. He stayed rooted in business language, citing timelines, data, and corporate processes. The facilitator gently interrupted and asked, "Yes, but how does it make you feel to hear her story?"

Still, the CEO answered with stoicism and facts. No emotion. No acknowledgment of her pain. No words that might begin to connect.

Finally, the facilitator took the microphone, and speaking for the room of over 200 business executives, said what had not yet been said and needed to be said: "We are all so sorry for your loss."

That moment revealed everything. Leadership is not just about what we know or how we defend our decisions. It is about how we show up in the face of humanity. And it starts with the words we choose. A single sentence in this situation could have changed everything.

How we use airtime reveals our mental filters. It shows how we perceive situations and what we believe is worth paying attention to. Clients who lead multibillion-dollar organizations often share that they find it increasingly difficult to relate to family and old friends: "The 'big problems' they discuss seem so minor compared to what I now handle and am responsible for; it is kind of hard to empathize."

What we think about becomes what we speak about, and what we say reveals where we are focused.

The same principles apply in leadership. How you use airtime matters. The language you use sets the tone. It tells others who you are, and it teaches others how to treat you and how to treat each other. Your words are not just commentary; they are quite literally creating the culture of your team or family daily. Use airtime and language to create the kind of connection, future, and world you most want, both at home and at work.

BIG IDEA #6: CONVERSATION IS LEADERSHIP

Conversations are not important to leadership—they are leadership.

The sheer number of books and articles on effective communication reflects just how essential—and how rare—this skill truly is among leaders. Titles like *Fierce Conversations, Difficult Conversations, Crucial Conversations,* and *Conversational Intelligence* exist because conversation is both an art and a discipline. These resources offer valuable tools for navigating the complexities of human interaction, helping leaders recognize the real conversation that needs to be had and then, how to address it more effectively in real time.

To lead well, we must understand what holds us back from fully engaging with others. We need to be aware of the deeper, often unspoken dialogue happening within ourselves. Only then can we ensure that we and the people we are speaking with are saying what truly needs to be said.

However, because so much happens within any interaction, it can be difficult for even the best among us to process everything. As a result, we frequently realize that we didn't address the real issue long after a conversation ends.

While most conversations involve the simple exchange of information, some are of the caliber that could transform a decision, a relationship, an organization, or the world. Unfortunately, most conversations that could transform something don't. It is not that these conversations are not happening—they are. But too often, we end up having these conversations in our heads rather than with the people who really need to hear them.

On our commute home, for example, we find ourselves playing out a discussion from earlier in the day with a colleague in our mind. When we get home and relay the conversation to our partner, we share key points we failed to share with the person or people who could *actually* do something about them. We need to bring more of this internal dialogue out and into our real-world exchanges.

PRACTICE #6: LEARNING FROM YOUR CONVERSATIONS

Reflect on the conversations you had during this last week. Was one particularly difficult, demanding, or rewarding? What happened?

- Did you say everything that needed to be said?
- If you held back, notice what you failed to say and why.
- Where were you highly effective in your use of language or perhaps courageous to address your real thoughts, feelings, or concerns? Where did you miss the mark?

What advice do you have for yourself for future interactions?

ONE CONVERSATION. WALK AWAY EMPTY

A tool I often share to help clients bring more awareness into their conversations is called *One Conversation. Walk Away Empty.*

Let me clarify—I don't mean you should leave a conversation feeling emotionally drained. Quite the opposite; you should walk away feeling emotionally clear, like you've said what needed to be said, nothing more and nothing less. Walking away empty means you're not holding on to confusion, frustration, or questions you were too hesitant to ask.

Here's how this often plays out at work.

Imagine you and I are working together on a high-stakes project. During a status meeting, I mention that the client presentation needs to be reworked because the design hasn't been approved. You pause because you just spoke with the marketing lead yesterday, and you were told the design *was* approved. But instead of speaking up, a second conversation starts playing out in your mind: *Wait, that's not right. Should I correct her? Maybe she knows something I don't. I don't want to look like I'm challenging her authority.* So you stay quiet. Later, I find out the design *was* approved, and I'm left wondering why you didn't say anything. You walk away carrying uncertainty and self-doubt. I walk away with a false assumption and wasted time. No one wins.

Now imagine you make a different choice. You say, "Actually, I confirmed with marketing yesterday that the design was approved. Do you have different information?" That's it. A short moment of courage. The air is cleared, the project stays on track, and both of us walk away empty, meaning, with nothing left unresolved.

Here's a similar scenario at home. Imagine your partner comes home late again. They barely acknowledge you and go straight for their phone. You feel dismissed and hurt. But instead of saying anything, you think, *They must be stressed. I don't want to start a fight.* So you stay silent. The next day, you're short with them or emotionally distant. They're confused, and now there's tension between you. Once again, the real conversation, the one that mattered, never happened.

Now imagine this moment is handled differently. You wait until later that evening and say, "Hey, when you came in tonight and didn't say much to me, I felt a little dismissed. I know it's probably not what you intended, but I wanted to share how it felt." Your partner replies, "I'm really sorry. I had a rough day. The truth is I'm feeling overwhelmed with work right now."

Clarity. Reconnection.

At every turn, we face this choice: to speak what's true or to stay silent and carry the emotional weight. Sometimes, it's best to address things in the moment. Other times, especially when emotions run high, it's wiser to wait for a better time. There's no hard and fast rule. What matters most is becoming aware of the second conversation that arises in our mind and developing the courage to eventually bring it into the one conversation you have with others.

This might sound basic, but living it is another thing entirely. I can easily do this with my children because they are so gracious and open. However, I struggle to share my real thoughts and feelings with my husband as it can so easily be taken as a criticism and turn into an argument. So I know what I am asking of you. Again, I don't profess to be able to live all of this well, only that I am aware of the real work to be done.

Here's another common example. You're in a meeting with your boss, and she dismisses an idea you offered, saying, "That's not really a priority right now." But what you hear is "Your ideas aren't valuable." You feel deflated. After the meeting, you vent to a colleague, but you never raise it with your boss. Over time, you stop speaking up. The one conversation happened about project priorities, but the second, deeper one about respect and value never did. Months later, your disengagement is misread as a lack of interest or commitment.

Now imagine the same moment but handled differently. Later that day, you say to your boss, "Can I check something with you? In today's meeting, when you said my idea wasn't a priority, I found myself wondering if my contributions are valuable. I may be reading too much into it, but I wanted to ask directly." Your boss replies, "Oh, yes, they are 100%. I was focused on the deadline and didn't mean to shut down your idea. It is absolutely relevant for next quarter. I'm glad you asked. Can you raise it again at our next meeting so we don't lose sight of it?"

Now the air is clear. Trust is preserved. And you walk away with no need to replay the moment or vent to someone else. You addressed it directly.

Of course, you might also hear, "I'm glad you raised this. Yes, I do value your ideas. But here's what I need you to understand: You often bring up new suggestions after we've aligned on a direction, and it can derail the group's focus. In fast-paced meetings, especially when key stakeholders are present, like today, timing and audience matter. I want you to develop greater awareness of when to contribute and when to hold your ideas for a different setting. That kind of discernment will take your leadership to the next level. Got it?"

It's not always comfortable, but it is real. Having one conversation is about connecting on shared reality—not just your reality, not just mine, but a genuine exchange: "What's happening for you?" and "Here is what's happening for me." It creates understanding, greater alignment, and often, real growth.

To have one conversation so you can walk away empty, focus on this question: *What do I believe is in the best interests of the people I lead and the work I serve?*

By doing so, you'll know you did everything you could to foster an authentic exchange. Even if the interaction doesn't go as well as you hoped, you can be proud that you didn't avoid it. You pulled your seat fully up to the table and focused on connecting and being of service. And because there's nothing left unsaid, you'll feel proud knowing you were courageous and didn't cower because you were afraid.

On the other hand, when you hold back, you leave the interaction unsettled and are forced to carry your questions, concerns, and doubts. You may tell yourself you avoided discomfort, but what you really avoided was clarity.

Perhaps you have an important conversation pending right now, but because you anticipate it will be uncomfortable, you've been putting it off, hoping it will go away. You can certainly hope. However, important conversations tend not to go away. They simply go underground, where they quietly erode trust, clarity, and connection.

Real conversations, especially the hard ones, come with a cost. They may make you feel vulnerable, and there's always a risk they won't go well. But there's also a cost to not having them: diminished trust, growing resentment, poor results, and damaged relationships. As a rule, the longer you wait, the higher the price.

INTRODUCING REAL CONVERSATIONS: THE FIVE QUESTIONS WORKSHEET: A BUILD ON THE SELF-INQUIRY TOOL (SIT)

Leaders (that's you!) who work exceptionally well with and through others regularly have the real conversations they know they need to have. They do so directly, early, often, and with the right people.

To support this, I created a simple, yet powerful tool called *Real Conversations: The Five Questions Worksheet.* It builds on the SIT we used in chapter four to bring your inner beliefs and emotions to the surface. While the SIT helps uncover all that is playing out inside of you—your thoughts, feelings, assumptions, judgments, fears, and inner dialogue—the Five Questions Worksheet enables you to discern which parts of that internal experience are most important to share out loud. It helps you become aware of your full thinking and name the relevant data points that are shaping your perspective, which is often the very reason the conversation needs to happen in the first place. It also brings awareness to what might be holding you back from speaking up.

I use this worksheet with clients and teach it at offsites to help leaders hear themselves more clearly, identify the real conversation begging to be had, and prepare themselves to have that conversation. The tool makes it easier to get to the heart of what matters, so they can speak directly, stay in integrity, and walk away empty.

Here's the worksheet:

Real Conversations
The Five Questions Worksheet

The purpose of *The Five Questions Worksheet* is to speed up the time it takes for you to:

1. Recognize the real conversation begging to be had, and;
2. Ensure you can effectively have it in real time.

Your answers to these five questions will often be the exact conversation you need to have with the relevant person or people. Answer the questions and then consider your answers a script for the conversation, which you might even share verbatim.

1. What is *the situation*? What are the observable behaviors—mine and others'—in this situation?

2. What am I *thinking and feeling*? Am I mad, sad, frustrated, inspired, critical, judgmental, etc.?

3. *Why might I hold back* from having the real conversation playing out in my mind? What story am I telling myself that might limit what I say or do? What fears or concerns do I have about having this conversation?

4. *What do I want* to say and do? What do I believe is in the best interest of the people I lead and the business(es) I serve?

5. What *important impact* could the real conversation have on the relationship and/or the business? What is my intention in having it?

INNERLIFELEADERSHIP
SUSANNE BIRO INC.

Again, your answers to these five questions will often be the exact conversation you want and need to have with the person or people in question. Answer the questions and then consider your answers a script for the conversation, which you might even share verbatim.

Here's an example. One client told me about a high-performing team member, Sam, who consistently overprepared, worked long hours, and rarely delegated tasks. Through our discussion, my client realized that Sam's behavior was driven by a fear of failure, disappointing others, and not being enough. It was unsustainable and held Sam back from becoming the strategic leader my client needed Sam to be.

My client used the Five Questions Worksheet to plot out the conversation he knew he needed to have with Sam. Here's what it looked like:

1. What is the situation?
Sam consistently takes on too much work, resists delegating, and stays late most nights. I've observed this for months. Sam seems to carry the weight of every project, even when support is available. It's beginning to affect team dynamics and Sam's capacity to grow into more senior responsibilities.

2. What am I thinking and feeling?
I'm impressed by Sam's dedication, but I'm also concerned. I feel uneasy watching this pace continue. I'm worried Sam will burn out—or worse, get stuck in a pattern of being the doer rather than evolving into the strategic leader I know she can be. I feel some guilt that I haven't raised this sooner.

3. Why might I hold back from having the real conversation playing out in my mind?

I fear demotivating Sam or sounding ungrateful for the many times she went above and beyond to ensure we hit necessary milestones. The story I'm telling myself is that giving this feedback might make Sam feel criticized, and if I am honest, I am worried that without her always delivering above and beyond, future milestones will be missed. I also worry that Sam may not see this behavior as a problem, which could make the conversation awkward and change our great relationship.

4. What do I want to say/do?

I want to have the conversation directly. Sam deserves the truth so she can advance to the senior leadership roles she aspires to. What I most want to say...

"Sam, I've noticed how often you take on more than is reasonable—or even healthy. You work incredibly hard, and your standards are exceptional. But I believe this pattern, while it may have served you in the past, is now limiting your capacity to grow as a leader. I want you to know that I see your talent, your work ethic, and your potential. You are deeply valued here. And I believe you're capable of far more—but not by doing more, by leading differently. I want you to begin delegating more and coach and develop your team more fully. I'd also like you to consider what's driving this need to do it all yourself. Would you be open to working with a coach or mentor to explore that?"

5. What important impact could the real conversation have on the relationship/the business?

This conversation could unlock the next level of leadership for Sam. It could help prevent burnout, elevate team performance, and increase Sam's ability to focus on strategy rather than execution. For our relationship, it signals that I see and care about her and her ultimate success, not merely what she can do for me.

Having this conversation changed everything. Sam admitted that her fear of disappointing others had long driven her approach to work. And with this insight and feedback, Sam began taking concrete steps to delegate more, say no when appropriate, and redefine success as coaching and empowering others, not just delivering results personally.

The Five Questions Worksheet turned my client's internal concern into a supportive and strategic conversation, one that built trust, inspired growth, and served the business.

This is what real leadership looks like in practice.

"Hey, Sam, do you have 15 minutes? I want to talk about something I've been noticing.

You're someone I really respect—you take on a ton, your work ethic is exceptional, and you always deliver. But I've been watching this for a while, and I'm starting to feel uneasy. You're staying late most nights, taking on more than anyone could reasonably manage, and I'm worried it's not sustainable.

Here's the thing—I don't want to sound ungrateful because I genuinely appreciate and benefit from your dedication. But I think the very thing that's made you successful so far, this drive to do it all, will now hold you back. I see so much potential in you as a leader, but the next level for you isn't doing more; it's leading differently. That means delegating, empowering and coaching your team, and maybe even looking at what's behind your need to carry so much yourself.

Would you be open to exploring this with a coach or mentor? I think this shift could not only help you but also strengthen the entire team. I'm bringing this up because I care about you and your greatest success, not just what you can do working for me today. And I really believe this could be a turning point—not just in your role but in how you lead and experience life."

It's a clear example of how courageous, heartfelt conversations can unlock potential for both individuals and the entire organization.

TO COMMUNICATE, CONNECT ON A HUMAN LEVEL

Effective communication requires, first and foremost, that you connect with yourself. To communicate purposefully, you must first know what you care most about and why it matters. When you speak from that place, others feel it. Even when you're communicating with hundreds or thousands, what resonates is not just what you say but the humanity behind it. People connect to people, and both business and life are filled with people.

At the core, we all care about one thing: making life better in a way that matters.

Here is an example that illustrates what it sounds like to truly communicate on a human level:

A founder and CEO I coach was preparing to roll out a new leadership development program to his executive team. As he shared his early drafts with me, the plan was clear, well-structured, and action oriented, but it just sounded flat. So I asked him, "Where did you go? What I don't hear is why this matters so deeply to you, why you care that people have the opportunity to learn more about themselves."

Having people know themselves was central to this CEO's mission, a purpose that extended far beyond his company's services. He desperately wanted others to understand themselves so they could experience more connection, joy, and success. His desire for this reality was missing in what he shared with me.

I said, "Tell me again," and then I asked, "What is different about this program from all the others you have done?" He paused. He reconnected with himself and shared how he had spent most of his career running scared, struggling with ADHD, masking his limitations, and trying to outwork the fear that never left him. There was relentless pressure to perform while never letting others know of his struggles. But over time, he learned to tell the truth about himself and embrace his story. And in doing so, in learning more about himself, he granted himself freedom.

The next time he shared his presentation, his voice was shaking, "This program is about gifting that same kind of freedom to others." He wanted his leaders to feel their own brilliance and potential, embrace their own personal history and stories, and feel safe being open about their strengths and their limitations. He believed that by knowing themselves more deeply, they could lead with more authenticity, impact, and success.

Once he connected with himself, everything about how he communicated shifted. He led with his "why," shared his personal journey, and made clear the future he wanted to create with and for them. He used human language, acknowledged what had not worked in the past, and invited his team to something far more meaningful than just another leadership program. He was not just informing them, he was inspiring them—and as a result, they didn't just hear the message, they felt it.

That is the power of human communication.

APPLY THE IDEA

Before you can communicate with clarity and conviction, you must first connect with yourself. What you most want for your own life is often exactly what you most want to inspire in others. When you're clear on your "why," your communication becomes more meaningful, resonant, and effective.

Take a few quiet moments and reflect in your journal. Use these questions to uncover what truly matters to you and why:

- Why am I doing the work I'm doing?
- What do I care most about?
- Why does that matter so much to me?

- What have I struggled with or had to overcome that now fuels my desire to improve the world for others?
- If I could speak from my heart, what would I say about what I care about most and the future I hope we can create together?

Throughout this chapter, we've explored how to most effectively interact with others by bringing humanity and intention into your interactions. Whether you're speaking with a team, a family member, or anyone else, being thoughtful about your language and how you want to use limited airtime makes a big difference. By taking the time to understand yourself, your purpose, and the motivations behind your actions, you can focus on communicating more clearly and authentically. Your self-awareness and focused purpose will create more meaningful connections, so you get what we each crave most: to feel known and to feel like we know others.

CHAPTER SEVEN

TRUST IS EVERYTHING

In a world shaped by deepfakes, digital fraud, misinformation, and AI-generated deception, knowing what's real and who is real has never been more difficult or more essential. Surrounded by curated personas and surface-level interactions, we're constantly, often unconsciously, scanning for authenticity. *Who can I trust? What can I believe?*

These aren't peripheral concerns. They lie at the core of every decision we make, every relationship we build, and every risk we take. In this chapter, I'll define exactly what trust is and why it matters, show you how to build (and rebuild) it, and break down what causes trust to erode and how to respond when it does.

BIG IDEA #7: TRUST ISN'T IMPORTANT. IT'S EVERYTHING.

Trust is the invisible thread that holds our world together. It underpins our financial systems, healthcare, education, and daily interactions. We believe that banks are solvent, doctors are competent, and universities provide learning and opportunity. We assume our leaders are qualified. We count on systems to enforce standards and protect us and our investments. We even trust that the driver speeding toward us will stay on their side of the yellow line.

Without trust, society, business—*everything*—falls apart.

Just as language is fundamental to communication, trust is foundational to leadership and life. It is the bedrock of all meaningful relationships. Trust enables people to collaborate, partnerships to flourish, and leaders to lead effectively.

Although many of us have had to deal with a boss who seemed to lack morals, empathy, or sincerity, most professionals are not compulsive liars and cheats, out to pull one over on the rest of us. Most are healthy, well-adjusted adults who've spent years working to contribute to their chosen profession and industry. They are often highly educated, experienced, and competent, and they want to do the right thing.

These professionals are people like *you*.

Why, then, does a lack of trust plague so many relationships, teams, departments, and organizations?

As we work with others, we may experience negative feelings about them and come to realize those feelings are rooted in trust or a lack of it. Do any of these thoughts sound familiar?

- "We can't count on the sales team."
- "He is so frustrating to deal with."
- "I don't like her."

While you may, indeed, be frustrated with or simply not like someone, quite often those feelings stem from the fact that the person hasn't demonstrated their trustworthiness, or worse, they have shown themselves to be untrustworthy.

- "We can't count on the sales team because I don't trust that they know our product well enough."
- "He is so frustrating to deal with because I don't trust him to follow through."
- "I don't like her because I don't trust that she has my best interests at heart."

When we can't count on the people around us, we stop delegating, start second-guessing decisions, or feel the need to double-check everything (aka micromanage). At worst, we look for ways to work around them and prepare to protect ourselves if things go, as we anticipate they will, sideways.

But when we know there are people and processes we can rely on, we're freed up to focus, deliver, and innovate.

We often think of trust as binary: Either I trust you or I don't. But trust is more complex.

I can trust your intention to do great work but perhaps not your competence. Or I might trust your skills and ability but not your reliability to come through for me when you say you will: "He is the best, but he takes forever to get things done." Or maybe I trust your skills and follow-through, but I fear you only care about yourself: "I doubt she will tell the board this was my idea."

Thus, we might think of trust in terms of the following:

- **Competence:** Do I trust you have the talent, knowledge, network, and/or skills to deliver what you say you can?
- **Reliability:** Do I trust you will do what you say you'll do, when you say you'll do it?
- **Intention:** Do I trust you care about me and my ultimate success?

We can each behave in ways that build trust and in ways that break it. Our everyday actions, as well as our general attitude and behaviors, teach others how trustworthy we are.

HOW WE BUILD TRUST

Trust is built through consistent, authentic, and accountable behavior. It's not created in grand gestures but in the small actions we demonstrate daily.

Let's look at everyday actions that earn and reinforce trust:

- Showing up prepared and on time
- Doing what you say you will do
- Genuinely supporting the success of others
- Acknowledging and addressing the questions others ask of us
- Taking responsibility for results, including mistakes and failures
- Giving credit where credit is due

Trust really can be built very quickly, often within the first few seconds of a conversation. When I first meet with a potential client, I know I have no more than 15 to 30 seconds to establish credibility, connection, and a sense of safety. I'm ready and waiting before the video call begins, fully present and free of distractions. I have usually spent several hours researching the client and company so I feel confident and aware. I begin by sharing something personal and relevant to who they are and why we're meeting, not as small talk but to create a real human connection. I then lead with a single, sincere question: "How can I be most helpful to you in our time today?"

My focus is entirely on the other person. I don't speak about myself unnecessarily, recite my resume, or try to sell or impress. Everything I offer is in service to them—what they need, care about, or are working through—whether we work together or not. I see it as a privilege to earn someone's trust, and I treat every moment of their time with deep respect.

Of course, trust also builds over time. It's shaped not just by first impressions but by consistent signals we receive repeatedly. Over time, consistent behaviors form patterns, and patterns are, ultimately, what shape belief.

TRUST BEGINS WITH PATTERNS

One way to understand trust is through the lens of patterns.

- The first time something happens, it's an incident: *"Hmm, that is interesting."*
- If it happens again, it becomes a coincidence: *"Hey, there it is again."*
- By the third time, it becomes a pattern, and that pattern shapes belief: *"This is who this person is."*

When the pattern reflects reliability, competence, and good intentions, trust is formed and deepened.

Let's look at this from a non-business perspective.

Incident: I recently visited a new doctor. I tend to feel anxious in medical settings (perhaps it's because I'm wearing a paper garment with the back open!), but when the doctor entered the room, he greeted me with a warm smile and a thoughtful introduction. I immediately felt more at ease. *He feels like a good man.*

Coincidence: He mentioned that he and his wife had been running the practice for over 30 years. That statement communicated stability and experience. *Oh, great, he knows what he's doing,* I thought. *He is fully competent.*

Pattern: Finally, he shared something personal about his own life, creating a genuine human connection. We were speaking person to person, not just doctor to patient. *How great that he and his wife are focusing on the same things my husband and I are.*

In just three small moments, I felt something rare in the healthcare system: I felt safe, understood, and respected.

Of course, trust can erode just as quickly. Let's look at this from a business perspective.

Incident: You schedule your first meeting with a peer who leads another business unit that you need to partner with on a key project. He arrives a few minutes late to the meeting, and while you tell yourself it's no big deal, he doesn't acknowledge the delay or offer a simple "Sorry I'm late."

Coincidence: The next time, he's late again, not on camera, and seems distracted. He asks questions you've already answered by email. You think: *Okay, this is frustrating. I sent him these answers yesterday.*

Pattern: By the third meeting, he hasn't done what he said he would. At this point, you're not really surprised. *I knew he would drop the ball.*

Now there's a pattern, and with it, a belief. You form a clear impression not only of him but possibly of his entire team or department. A red flag rises in your mind, warning you to stay cautious and maybe even steer clear of this team for future projects.

Trust rarely breaks in a single moment. It erodes gradually, through a series of small but consistent signals. When someone repeatedly shows up unprepared, your mind forms conclusions about their reliability, competence, and intent. Your belief about who they are solidifies, and that belief determines whether you want to continue investing in them or start to pull away. This is how our reputations are built. It is also how brands are built or falter.

First impressions matter, but so does what comes next. Getting those first 15 to 30 seconds of a conversation right sets the tone for a great connection. But if I fumble in that first minute or even on the first day of a new collaboration, we haven't lost our chance. People are surprisingly forgiving when I show up with honesty and humility. I've seen time and again how a relationship can turn around simply by being honest and demonstrating a genuine desire to serve.

So as you meet new individuals, offer them the grace to be human: to occasionally stumble and course correct. At some point, you'll need someone to offer the same grace to you. At the same time, never ignore what your gut is telling you. A single incident may be a fluke, but once you see a pattern that involves a lack of genuineness and integrity, you know who someone truly is. Get good at listening to your intuition and trusting it quicker.

TRUST IS ACCOUNTABILITY PERSONIFIED

What does it mean to hold yourself accountable?

It means taking ownership of your actions and all of your results. It means acknowledging mistakes, learning from what went wrong, and becoming better as a result. Sometimes, it also means facing the difficult truth that you were the reason something failed.

A senior executive I worked with was facing a key turnover and growing dysfunction on his senior leadership team. He came to coaching frustrated, blaming people for being disengaged and resistant. As we explored the situation, he began to see the role he played. He had shifted priorities without sufficient communication, failed to acknowledge contributions, and only offered feedback when something went wrong. The team wasn't dysfunctional; they were confused and felt unappreciated.

To turn the situation around, he took responsibility for his role and addressed the issue openly. "I've never been great at noticing all that is being done well, but I need to get better at voicing this so that this chapter in our careers doesn't feel like just one damned problem after another." He then named key successes achieved by specific individuals before focusing the team on the next set of challenges they needed to address. He communicated more frequently and more fully and began ending meetings with one simple question: "What do you most need from me this week?"

The change was noticeable. Retention stabilized, morale lifted, and performance increased—not because his team changed, but because he did.

When things fall apart, it's easy to look outward. But in leadership, there is no "them."

They are your team. You are responsible.

If your team is underperforming or results are lacking, that's your cue to take a closer look at your own leadership. Your job is to ensure the right people are in the right roles and they are aligned, engaged, supported, and equipped to do the work of their lives and succeed.

When outcomes fall short, you must ask yourself important questions:

- How do I own this?
- What must I do next?
- What is it that only I can do?

Great leaders (partners, spouses, parents, friends) don't deflect. They don't delay. They take responsibility. And when they do, accountability sounds like this:

- "If this change is going to be successful, it has to start with me,"
- "I need to become better," and
- "I own this, and I'll work to make it right."

One of the most powerful ways that we demonstrate accountability, building trust in the process, is through the language we choose. Even a single word can reveal whether we're stepping up to lead or stepping away. This is what I call the "Power of I."

THE POWER OF I

The word "I" is essential to accepting accountability. Using "I" forces you to take responsibility for what you're experiencing. It forces you to own it.

Listen to others speak, and one of the first things you will notice is how often people use words like "we," "you," "one," or "they" when they are really talking about *themselves*.

Examples include the following:

- We are getting frustrated.
- You try to connect with millennials, but…
- If one hasn't bought into the idea, then…
- They might not trust him.

One of the smallest and most powerful changes we can make to significantly improve our communication is to replace those four words with "I."

Consider the following:

- I am getting frustrated…
- I try to connect with millennials, but…
- I have not bought into the idea, so…
- I don't trust him…

This one simple change makes a big difference, and it has a significant payoff.

Take me, for instance. When I speak from my own experience, my listeners experience me as more authentic, transparent, and often, trustworthy. These are all qualities we seek and expect from those we work with and through. Using "I" creates more trust because it is a more honest way to communicate.

For example, I used to use the word "one" often. It would sound like this: "One can get really frustrated when colleagues are not performing, and no one is calling them on it." When I change "one" to "I," it becomes: "I get really frustrated when colleagues are not performing, and I am not calling them on it."

See how the latter is more honest and requires me to hold myself accountable for acting?

In using the word "I," I no longer hide behind vague identities like "one." Instead, I immediately take ownership and accountability by being specific about what is occurring for me. Using the word "I" gives my listener or listeners and myself direct access to exactly where I stand and what I think and/or feel.

The word "I," although more authentic, powerful, and effective, is rarely used in the way I suggest. Why? Because it is riskier. When I use "I" instead of "one," it requires me to name and own my honest thoughts and feelings, which I might not even be fully aware of—or if I am, I'm not yet ready or willing to share with others.

Using "I" requires me to be vulnerable because it demands I ask for what I want or need, something surprisingly few of us human beings are comfortable doing. "I have not bought into the idea, so I would like us to all take a step back. I can feel the group wanting to move forward. However, there are red flags I just can't get over. Can we all please discuss?"

PRACTICE #7: EMBRACING THE POWER OF "I"

As we discussed in the previous chapter, the way we use language has a direct impact on how others perceive our integrity and willingness to be accountable. When we avoid using "I," we also avoid responsibility. We distance ourselves from our own opinions, emotions, and decisions. But when we use "I" intentionally, we lead with clarity and ownership. We create trust. Our teams are more likely to follow a leader who is honest about their experience, even when it's difficult.

This exercise helps you become aware of how language either supports or erodes trust in those you lead.

Week 1: Observe Others

This week, listen closely as others speak—in meetings, during conference calls, at the coffee shop, and with family members at home. Pay special attention to how people naturally, unconsciously (or subconsciously) remove themselves from being seen, taking ownership, being accountable, or being vulnerable. Watch for words like "we," "you," "one," or "they" when you can tell from the context of the conversation that they are speaking of their own experience and really mean "I."

First, notice this in others, and then notice how it affects the trust you have in them.

Week 2: Turn the Lens Inward

Now begin noticing your own language. Do you use "we," "you," "one," or "they" when you really mean "I"? It may be hard to catch this in yourself at first; that's normal. Most of us are blind to our own patterns of speech and the deeper implications they carry. Try partnering with a trusted colleague or friend and holding each other accountable. Gently point out when you hear one another default to vague or distancing language.

As you become more aware, begin choosing "I" whenever you're speaking from your own experience. It may feel vulnerable at first. *Do it anyway.*

Notice the impact of making this one small but powerful change. Notice how it makes you feel. Notice how it is a more honest way of communicating and how it builds more trust.

HOW WE BREAK TRUST

We can each break trust daily without any awareness that we are doing so. If you hold a powerful position, whether as CEO or parent, few will be brave enough to let you know when this happens. But don't deceive yourself: The people around you see everything, and they are constantly assessing you (especially teenagers, if you have them!).

When we act in political, petty, unprofessional, or childish ways, it breaks trust with our colleagues and employees, and it hurts our ability to succeed. For example, gossiping about a teammate instead of addressing issues directly, rolling our eyes in meetings, withholding information to gain an advantage, or shutting down when we don't get our way are seemingly small behaviors, but they erode trust.

To lead our world well, we must become the kind of leader we seek: We must care about the personal well-being and professional success of others as much as we care about our own.

We must become the kind of person and professional we most appreciate, a human that can be trusted in all ways— our intentions, our competence, and our reliability to follow through.

We have all seen how one careless act can destroy an entire career or decades of trust: a CEO makes an offensive comment on social media, triggering public backlash and a sharp decline in brand value, or a senior team member loses their temper in a meeting, humiliates a colleague, and damages relationships that took years to build. In both cases, a single moment of poor judgment can undo years of hard work and credibility. Perhaps you recall how a parent did this to you in your youth, leading to resentment you may still hold.

Of course, some corporate executives have notoriously broken trust, leading to serious consequences for themselves and their organizations. But often, trust is not broken in big, obvious, illegal, or immoral ways, at least not by most of us. Instead, we erode trust in small, daily choices without fully appreciating the profound impact this has on our effectiveness and long-term success.

A common way we break trust is by providing negative feedback in public, often passive-aggressively. Doing so not only embarrasses the team member in question, but it also illustrates that the leader doesn't respect their team members. What's worse, it opens the field for gossip as the witnessing team members share and reshare the confrontation with other people in the organization. If a situation presents a meaningful learning opportunity for the whole team and can be addressed constructively in a group setting, consider having a pre-meeting with the person or people involved. Make sure they're on board and that the conversation won't shame or harm them. If there's any doubt or a risk it could go sideways, take it private.

Have you ever felt someone's grace when they had the power to hurt, diminish, or embarrass you publicly, but they instead pulled you aside and spoke with respect and care? If so, you know how deeply it stays with you. This is how trust is built and how relationships are strengthened. One act of grace in a hard moment is worth more than a thousand easy days.

I've worked with clients who came to understand how their leadership style was negatively affecting others. Some were let go and used the opportunity to reflect and grow before stepping into a new role. Others received candid feedback from a 360-degree review or were advised to engage a coach to address behaviors that undermined team culture, performance, key relationships, and morale.

This feedback rarely comes as a complete shock. Often, clients acknowledge the truth of what's shared; they simply hadn't grasped the full impact of their actions. One leader, for example, was surprised to learn he was known as "The Consultant," while another had earned the nickname "Teflon." The first was seen as someone who gave advice but avoided work, and the second was seen as someone who never took responsibility for their results. They called him Teflon because nothing ever stuck.

Trust for both leaders began to erode. When "The Consultant" spoke in meetings, subtle cues like eyerolls and exchanged glances signaled the team's growing frustration: "Here he goes again, advising but not doing anything to fix the issue." With "Teflon," it showed up in the way people stopped bringing him problems altogether. "What's the point?" one teammate said. "He's just going to deflect or blame someone else." Team members started solving issues via side conversations, leaving him out of the loop entirely.

In coaching sessions, several executives have admitted, "I don't actually think of myself as a leader." I replied to each, "That might be part of the problem." I added, "You have to think of yourself as a leader to act like one. People expect you to lead, not just advise." Of the most respected leaders, people often say, "She never asked us to do anything she wasn't willing to do herself. When things got tough, she was right there with us."

In each case, we focused on specific behavior shifts. A passive statement like "You guys need to handle this" became "We need to handle this. Let's identify what each of us will take on. I'll start by reaching out to the client to repair the relationship."

In these examples, the turning point was realizing that "the word on the street" matters; people notice everything. Holding yourself to the same standards you expect from others is essential, whether you're a parent pitching in at home or an EVP leading a global team.

These clients began rebuilding trust through honesty and transparency. They acknowledged the feedback, admitted to how it felt to hear it (hard for some, not surprising to others), and shared their commitment to making changes. One client said, "So, it turns out I have a nickname: Teflon. At first, I was embarrassed, but now I'm grateful. It made me realize I often leave meetings without clearly naming my responsibilities. Moving forward, I'll end every meeting by sharing my commitments. We're a team, and I'm part of it. Maybe I'll even earn a cooler nickname."

With candor, commitment, and a touch of humility and humor, these leaders demonstrated that trust cannot only be repaired but also strengthened.

REFLECT: THINK ABOUT A TIME WHEN SOMEONE BROKE TRUST WITH YOU.

- What happened?
- What impact did breaking trust have on your relationship? How did it change?
- What builds trust and breaks trust for you? Write this down, as it will often be what builds and breaks trust with others.

GHOSTING AND GASLIGHTING: WE NEED TO DO BETTER

Let's call out two trust-eroding behaviors, namely: ghosting and gaslighting. Both lessen relationships, credibility, and culture. And both are clear signs that we can and must do better.

GHOSTING: BEING CARELESS WITH OUR IMPACT

Ghosting is when a person avoids or disappears instead of addressing a difficult issue. It's either a lack of awareness or a refusal to engage genuinely. Whether intentional or not, it leaves people in confusion, frustration, and doubt. It happens when:

- a person dodges a tough topic or conversation;
- a colleague doesn't reply or fails to address the questions you asked; or
- a partner disappears without resolution or acknowledgment.

Ghosting occurs when we are unaware of just how much we matter. It also occurs when we are afraid to address what is uncomfortable. It leaves others to make up a story, and the story they make up usually isn't a good one. Ghosting also tells others, whether we intend it or not, that they don't matter and their contributions or concerns aren't important. It erodes the most precious currency we have: trust.

In business and in our personal relationships alike, ghosting often looks like this: you send a colleague an email with three clear questions that you need answers to in order to move a project forward. Or you ask a family member about three things that matter to you, like plans for the weekend, who will handle an errand, and how they're feeling about an upcoming event. The response you get touches only two of the questions and skips over the third. You're left to wonder: *Did they not notice? Do they not care? Am I not important enough to warrant a full reply?*

What we often forget is how much our words, or lack of them, matter. It doesn't take much to build trust, only a little additional awareness. Even saying, "I know you asked three questions. I can answer two now, and I'll address the third when we speak next," keeps the connection intact. It communicates respect, provides clarity, and reminds others that they matter.

GASLIGHTING: WHAT DECEIVERS DO

If ghosting is passive, gaslighting is active. It's when a person twists reality to avoid accountability and make others doubt their own perception of events. Gaslighting generally denies the experience of others, and it can sound like:

- "That's not what happened,"
- "You're too sensitive,"
- "You misunderstood," and
- "You're making a big deal out of nothing."

Gaslighting distorts the truth and shifts the blame. It leaves people second-guessing themselves instead of trusting their own experience as relevant and valid.

Gaslighting erodes confidence, trust, and psychological safety. And once you lose those, you lose everything that makes a team of people great: honesty, the ability to connect on shared reality, ownership, innovation, and trust.

YOU DON'T GET AWAY WITH IT

The truth is that no one gets away with ghosting or gaslighting. Everyone notices. People see what you do, and they especially notice the patterns you follow. We are constantly observing one another, looking for evidence of who is genuine and who is putting on a performance and for what purpose. Your reputation is shaped every day by your actions, especially by how you handle yourself when things get difficult.

Consider this story:

During a high-stakes product launch, a senior manager realized her team was overloaded. She could have silently shifted work, ignored complaints, or let the stress build. Instead, she paused for five minutes, gathered the team, and said:

"I see the stress, and I'm adjusting priorities. We'll redistribute some tasks so no one burns out. If you need support along the way, I'm here."

That brief conversation cost her almost no time but demonstrated courage, thoughtfulness, and respect. People noticed. Morale stayed high and trust deepened. Small acts like this often have a bigger impact than grand gestures ever could.

Business, at its best, exists to make human life better. And how we conduct ourselves in business should reflect that principle. Too often, we make life hell for one another in the name of making the world better. It doesn't make sense.

Ghosting and gaslighting have no place in leadership. They erode trust and signal that values like character, honesty, and integrity are optional. If you say you care about people, prove it in how you treat them, especially when it's inconvenient or difficult.

You cannot claim to lead with integrity while ignoring emails, dodging hard conversations, or twisting facts to protect your ego. Trust is built in how you do everything. It's built on the respect you show for the people right in front of you. Every interaction is a chance to strengthen relationships or weaken them.

WE ARE ALWAYS BECOMING

The truth is that we never escape the inner shame we feel when we behave poorly. We either confront those parts of ourselves and grow, or we keep repeating the same patterns in different rooms, with different people, duplicating the same mistakes and wondering why we can't get ahead or our teams won't follow us.

Growth begins the moment we take responsibility for the impact we have on others, even unintentionally. Often, we just don't realize how much we matter to other people. Remember, you are kind of a big deal to the people you work with and through at work and at home. You are more powerful than you know.

We have all been on the receiving end of some ineffective leadership, as there is no such thing as a perfect leader. When we find ourselves in that position, it is time for us to extend grace to those above us. They are human beings, often striving to do their best in a very demanding role.

It is also time to be brave and have the real conversation with supervisors as readily as we have with direct reports, as we have a role to play in helping our leaders become the very best they can and need to be.

When integrity is lacking, it is essential to voice this, challenge it, and if nothing changes, end the relationship. Never stay where there is a lack of integrity.

Trust is the invisible currency of leadership. Without it, nothing works. With it, everything becomes possible (and fun!).

In the next chapter, I'll show you how to use the Big Ideas I've shared with you to evolve your leadership skills into coaching skills.

CHAPTER EIGHT

COACHING AND DEVELOPING OTHERS

There's a realization that comes for everyone at some point in life. For some, it might be the first moment of solitude after a long day. For others, it might be the day after their big "win," when they sit alone in their home and life doesn't feel all that much different. Or for others still, it might be at 4:00 a.m. and shows up in the form of a racing mind that can't get back to sleep. It's the moment we find ourselves saying: *This can't be all there is.* The deadlines, the titles, the business wins—they're not enough. They don't answer the questions brewing beneath the surface: *Who am I? What really matters?*

For many leaders, the answer begins with something unexpected: learning to coach. It comes when they begin to understand that coaching is so much more than a skillset; it is a way of thinking, a way of being, and ultimately, a way to reconnect with their core self.

About 20 years ago, I witnessed leaders experience this realization time and again. I was traveling the world teaching a course I had developed and written, working with business executives from Munich, Germany, to Macau, China, on how to coach for performance. At each conference, room after room was filled with committed professionals, each seeking better results for their team, their company, and if they dared admit it, for themselves.

And time after time, I saw a remarkable shift. As leaders began to see coaching not as a set of techniques but rather as a way of being and a way of thinking, conversations became more courageous and effective. There was something deeper happening: Leaders began to see themselves for who they truly were. *They began to reconnect with themselves.* They started to understand how their inner world was shaping their outer world, including their achievements, relationships, and reputation.

And once they saw that, they couldn't *unsee* it.

BIG IDEA #8: COACHING IS A MIRROR AND A CATALYST

For these leaders, coaching became the answer to those questions echoing beneath the surface. That's the thing about developing others: It's both a mirror and a catalyst. It reflects who we are today and stirs a powerful desire to become more—not just for ourselves but for others. We begin to understand that our role is not just to lead; it's to lift—not just to succeed but to help others win.

That kind of transformation doesn't begin with tactics or strategies—it begins with self-awareness. Before we can truly develop others, we have to look within and understand what's driving us. We often think that leadership begins with external or technical attributes, such as vision, strategies, goals, or competencies. However, what truly shapes a leader is their *inner life*—their thoughts, beliefs, emotions, intentions, and perspectives on the world.

Early in my career, I noticed something curious: Two leaders with nearly identical responsibilities, experience, and resources could create wildly different results. The difference wasn't in their intelligence or their ambition. It was in how they *thought*. One was reactive and often ruled by fear and a need to control, gain, or otherwise win over others. The other was reflective, deeply aware of what they wanted to give and how their presence impacted those around them.

One leader unknowingly created stress. The other created safety and, from there, forged inspiration and performance.

By observing the contrast between two leaders, I came to understand that performance starts with *consciousness*.

That's why coaching is so effective. Coaching helps people ask more effective questions. It interrupts automatic behavior. It creates space for people to share their dreams of who they want to be and what matters most to them. It builds safety and trust. And over time, it creates a culture where people grow, have ownership, and perform at their best—not because they're being pushed to produce but because they feel seen, heard, encouraged, and supported.

I WANT YOU TO WIN!

For well over a decade, I designed learning programs and taught leaders around the world how to coach for performance and lead with a coaching mindset. In other words, I've helped leaders reconnect with themselves, improve their lives and their own performance, and as a result, improve their ability to enhance the performance and lives of others. Once we achieve any version of success, the first thing we want to do is help others do the same! Now, that's a beautiful thing!

What I'm about to share with you is the very best of what I taught during that time. The ideas on these pages have been tested by thousands of leaders across industries, countries, and cultures.

Jonathan was one such leader, an executive at a large medical company. Jonathan was a natural coach—present, curious, and deeply committed to helping others grow. He has since passed, and I miss him immensely. He was one of the greatest people I had the pleasure of knowing and working with. His belief in others was unmistakable, and I often think of him when I reflect on the power of coaching done well.

It's people like Jonathan who remind me that there are great men and women at the helm of so many organizations. Whether you're a leader, parent, mentor, or friend, when you show up with a coaching mindset, you make people better. You help them see who they are, who they can be, and how to bridge that gap with courage and intention.

By using the tools I'm presenting in this chapter, you'll be able to:

- listen in a way that transforms conversations,
- ask questions that ignite ownership and insight,
- hold space for accountability *and* compassion, and
- know when to speak, when to wait, and how to build trust in every interaction.

These are not just coaching tools. They are *life* tools, and when you practice them—when you *really* live them—you become a better leader. More than that, you become someone others remember as the reason they finally saw what was possible for themselves. That's the power of coach-like leadership.

REACH YOUR NEXT LEVEL: FIRST, COACH YOURSELF

Before we can serve as mirrors or catalysts for others, we must be willing to hold up the mirror to ourselves. The first concept I want you to understand is that our ability to coach and develop others begins with our own commitment to growth.

You earn the right to coach others to *their* next level only by advancing yourself to *yours*. Coach is not a title you give yourself; it's a level of trust and respect others grant you when they see evidence of your skill, character, and consistent results.

You become a coach in the eyes of others by the way you live your life, lead your work, and pursue your own development. People are watching. They see your choices, your consistency, your follow-through, and your resilience. They choose who they will allow to influence them based on what they see and experience from you.

If you want to be a leader who helps others fulfill their potential, you must be actively doing the same for yourself. That is the foundation of authentic, effective coaching.

PRACTICE #8: STEPPING INTO YOUR NEXT LEVEL OF LEADERSHIP

Reflect on what it means for *you* to lead more powerfully. Your next level might include:

- being a more concise and effective communicator;
- inspiring others through your public speaking or storytelling;
- becoming more confident and influential in sales, marketing, or negotiation;
- strengthening your decisiveness and strategic thinking;
- becoming more skilled at coaching and developing others;
- gaining confidence in your financial, operational, or technical acumen;
- expanding your ability to network, influence, and promote ideas and people; and
- leading with greater courage, clarity, or conviction.

I once worked with a COO preparing to step into the CEO role who realized his next level wasn't about acquiring more technical expertise. It was about becoming a more inspiring communicator. While brilliant behind the scenes, he often lost his audience when speaking in high-stakes environments. He shared too many ideas and words, and it was hard to follow what was important from what wasn't. He committed himself to becoming a gifted storyteller and sought weekly feedback on his message and delivery. Within six months, not only had his board taken notice, but so had his team. He had earned the right to influence more broadly because he did the internal and external work to become masterful at his own communication.

Stories like his show what's possible when we choose to grow with intention. Now it's your turn to define what your next level looks like *and* commit to reaching it.

Ask yourself:

- What are your organization's three most important business imperatives this year?
- What are the corresponding leadership challenges and opportunities you face?
- What one to two changes in your personal leadership are necessary and have the potential to have the most significant impact?
- If you made these changes, what would be different in three months, six months? A year? How will you measure your success precisely and by what metrics?

This is now your own Personal Development Plan for the year.

EVOLVING FROM LEADER TO COACH

As you commit to your own next level, something powerful happens: You begin to see more clearly what others are capable of too. The inner work you do builds the foundation for outer impact. When I first started teaching coaching skills, I wasn't trying to turn leaders into coaches. I was trying to help them become more effective leaders. However, it turns out that the two aren't that different.

To coach is to care, listen deeply, speak honestly, and stay curious. Coaching is the practice of helping others become more self-aware, resourceful, and capable, something every leader wants for their people (and parents for their children), whether they realize it or not.

Over the years, as I taught this material, a pattern emerged. Leaders would take the course, try the tools, and within weeks, they'd come back saying things like the following:

- "My one-on-ones are completely different now."
- "I'm getting more insight into barriers that block my team's success in five minutes than I used to get in an hour."
- "My teenager actually opened up to me last night."

That's when I knew this work belongs everywhere—not just in performance reviews, but in tough client meetings, boardrooms, and dinner conversations, and at kitchen tables.

GETTING STARTED AS A COACH: USE YOUR EXPERIENCE AS A FOUNDATION

Before you can fully embrace coaching as a leader, it helps to reflect on how it's shown up in your own life. Chances are that someone has already played that role for you, and you can use that experience as your foundation.

I'd like to ask you some questions I've asked thousands of leaders: Who was one of your own best coaches? Who is someone who had a significant and positive impact on you becoming the person and professional you are today?

Think of someone who helped shape the path you're on. You might not have called them a coach at the time, but looking back, they changed what you believed about yourself or what you thought was possible. Maybe it was a math teacher, sports coach, music instructor, or manager at your first job. What was the nature of the relationship they created with you? Is there something they said or did that you still remember because it shifted how you saw yourself or your future?

One of my great coaches was my mom. She was loving and honest, and she often told me, "You can do anything you set your mind to." She chased her own dreams, stood up for herself, and did things that scared her—like starting a business at age 40. As she dared me to become more, I watched her do the same. She would often challenge my direct nature with a simple, gentle request: "Do it with more love." That one sentence might be responsible for every success I have today.

I dedicated my TEDx Talk, *Leadership: Lessons Learned in a Barber Shop,* to her for always believing in me, telling me the truth, challenging my poor behavior, and pushing me to pursue what I genuinely wanted. She loved me fiercely and taught me the power of that kind of love. I wouldn't be who I am today without her words—words that slowly became my own internal dialogue: *Do it with more love. You can do anything you set your mind to.*

I've heard countless stories about mothers and fathers, aunts and uncles, grandparents, teachers, sports coaches, dance instructors, first bosses, and even current supervisors (though I hear this last one less often than I'd like).

When I ask leaders to describe the nature of the relationship they had with this person and what their coach said or did that changed who they believed they were or what they thought was possible, the answers are strikingly similar:

- "They focused on me and my potential. They believed in me and cared deeply about my success. They loved me enough to confront me with my strengths and my weaknesses."
- "They were relentless in helping me grow. They were selfless and generous. They challenged me and championed me. They created visibility and opened doors."
- "They never gave up on me. They wanted my personal and professional success. I am who I am today, in large part, because of them."

When I hear stories like these, I often say, "Wonderful. I have nothing more to teach you about coaching. You already know what it is. You have only one task: Become that person for others."

So now I ask you:

- Who was one of your great coaches?
- What was the nature of the relationship they built with you?

- What is one thing they said or did that had a lasting impact—something that changed how you saw yourself or what you believed was possible?

And if no one comes to mind, I'm genuinely sorry—because everyone deserves a coach like that. But if you didn't have one, imagine who you would have wanted. What kind of relationship would have made all the difference for you? What would they have said or done to help you become the best version of yourself?

Whether you had a great coach or discovered the value of coaching by feeling its absence, by experiencing what *not* to do, you already know what great coaching looks and feels like. You only need to imagine the kind of person you had or wish you'd had, and then work to be that person in the lives of others.

CREATING YOUR COACHING GUIDE

One of the most powerful ways to embody great coaching is to create your own Coaching Guide. It will become a personal blueprint based on the people who helped shape you and the qualities you want to model for others.

I was fortunate to have several exceptionally great coaches in my life—my parents and a man named John Rose.

John was a longtime hair client (from the job I held in my mother's barbershop for 13 years, which I did to put myself through school), who also happened to be the president of Nuheat Industries, a company he had taken over and successfully grown. We'd meet about once a month at a restaurant, White Spot, in downtown Vancouver.

I remember proudly telling him I had joined a coaching company and handing him my new business card, expecting him to be impressed.

He wasn't.

He glanced at it, handed it back, and said, "I'll wait for the card that says Susanne Biro."

I was mad. I had worked so hard just to get that far. But as I drove home that morning, I realized what I was really upset about was the fact that I knew he was right.

In that one sentence, he made me realize that I didn't need to hide behind someone else's name. That I was good enough—capable enough—to stand fully on my own.

His words and actions stayed with me, as the words of a great coach often do. They echoed in my mind until the day I finally accepted the truth: I didn't need anyone else's logo to be legitimate. I was already enough. I ended up launching on my own and was more successful than I could have ever imagined. And as a great coach, John was the first to bring me into his company and refer me to others. We are friends to this day.

So when I think about what makes a great coach, I think of people like John and my parents and how they showed up for me.

My coaches:

- believed in me and my potential;
- told me the truth with respect and love;
- challenged me to become my best and highest self;

- cared about my ultimate success, no matter what it meant for them;
- created opportunities for me; and
- pursued their own dreams and success, inspiring me to do the same.

They each genuinely cared about me and my success. They wanted me to succeed in both business and life.

So to be an exceptional leader, coach, teacher, parent, or friend, I know I need to embody those same principles my coaches modeled for me.

That's my Coaching Guide. Now it's time to create yours.

REFLECT: ON YOUR BEST COACHES

Write down five or six coaching behaviors that worked or would have worked for you. Reflect on what it was about those behaviors that made a significant difference in your life. Again, if no great coach comes to mind, consider the ineffective coaches you've encountered—those who made you feel small, limited, or unseen. What did they do wrong? Write down the opposite of those behaviors, and let those lessons shape the kind of coach and leader you want to be and will be.

Once you've identified and written down those positive traits, consider the following:

- Post your Coaching Guide where you will see it every day.
- Revisit it each morning and allow it to guide your actions, conversations, and leadership decisions.

Living your Coaching Guide will help you become a more effective coach and leader both at work and in your personal life. The more you live by these principles, the greater your impact will be.

Speaking of impact, when you're clear on the kind of coach and leader you want to be, you'll start to notice how your presence affects others. After all, it's not just about what you do; it's about how others experience you. A big part of that experience is shaped by your mindset: the thoughts, assumptions, and beliefs you carry into each interaction. Let's talk about how your attitude doesn't just affect how you show up; it also shapes how people respond to you.

YOUR MINDSET SHAPES YOUR RELATIONSHIPS: THE A PLAYER EFFECT

Take a moment and remember the people you've worked with throughout your life. What did they think of you? Did they believe in your potential? Were they annoyed by you? Did they dismiss you or invest in you?

Chances are that you knew exactly how they felt. You could tell by the words they used, their tone of voice, the way they looked at you, or even how they stood when speaking to you. Their true opinion was never really hidden.

And the same is true for you. The people you work with today know exactly what you think about them—whether you're aware of it or not.

The way you think about someone influences how you treat them. And how you treat them impacts how they show up. Your thoughts become a self-fulfilling prophecy.

If you expect someone to be disengaged, you may withhold your enthusiasm or overlook their contributions. Sensing your lack of belief, they may shut down or grow defensive, reinforcing your original belief.

But what if your thoughts are the starting point of that cycle? What if the way you see someone—your assumptions about their ability, attitude, or potential—sets the entire tone for how you engage with them? Even before they speak or act, your mindset is already shaping the interaction. And in response to your subtle cues—your tone, your availability, your body language—they begin to behave in ways that confirm your original belief.

Think about the people you consider your "A Players"—those top performers you trust, enjoy, and rely on.

What qualities come to mind?

Most people describe A Players as competent, responsible, engaged, and self-aware. They're collaborative, proactive, and often a joy to be around. When you see them in the hallway or on video, you smile. You're quick to help, respond to their ideas, and advocate for their success. You expect great things from them—and they rise to meet those expectations.

Now think about your B Players—those who frustrate you, underperform, or simply haven't earned your confidence.

How do you behave around them?

Do you avoid eye contact? Let their emails sit unread a little longer? Hold back your full support? Quietly expect them to fail? You may not realize you do this, but they do. These people you subconsciously consider B Players feel the subtle cues you send, and they often live down to the expectations you've set for them.

When people sense that you don't think highly of them, they tend to respond in one of two ways:

- They try to prove themselves, which can show up as arrogance, anxiety, or neediness.
- They retreat, becoming distant, resentful, or disengaged.

Neither dynamic is productive, and neither leads to the kind of high-performing, trusting relationships you want on your team.

So what should you take away from this? *Your private thoughts aren't private.*

What you believe about others shapes how you lead them. And how you lead them shapes how they perform.

APPLY THE IDEA: REFRAME JUST ONE PERSON

Try this: Choose someone you've mentally labeled a B Player. For the next month, consciously treat them like an A Player. Speak to them with the same respect, openness, and candor you reserve for your top performers.

Be willing to be wrong about them. Suspend judgment. Stay curious. Look for their strengths. Voice your coaching on how they need to improve.

We are naturally more generous, collaborative, and candid with those we think highly of—so start thinking highly. You might be surprised at what changes.

And if you're stuck, revisit your Coaching Guide. Care about their success and be honest about what you notice and believe is necessary for their greatest success.

This one switch could change everything. Do this consistently and notice the results. At the end of the month, you'll be surprised by the positive changes that occur, not only in your team member but also in how they respond to you. They will either rise, or you will learn they can't or won't and then you can have that conversation.

Your ability to coach others depends on your willingness to do the hard work of growing yourself and on your ability to genuinely believe in the people around you. To tell them: *I see your potential, and I'm committed to helping you realize it.*

SHOW YOUR TEAM HOW TO REACH THEIR NEXT LEVEL

Of course, the A and B Players aren't the only people you will interact with. Consider everyone else you work closely with, including direct reports, peers, supervisors, board members, vendors, clients, and even family members. You work with and through these people every day to lead your life and business.

Let's take the previous exercise a step further. Who are the five people who, if they consistently performed at their best, would have the most significant positive impact on you and your business, work, or life? Identify them in your mind. Now ask yourself these questions:

- What is *their* next level?
- What strengths can they build on?
- What development opportunities would really assist them?
- How can you support, encourage, or challenge them?

To coach others to their next level, you must first *see* it. To see it, you must think about each person and their greatest future success.

APPLY THE IDEA: FOCUS MORE ON OTHERS

Given your answers to the above, identify one action you can do today to advance at least one of those five people.

Further, focus on others more than you might otherwise this week. Ask the people around you, such as your family, peers, and boss, what they need, and/or acknowledge their dedication, efforts, and work. Remember the five people you identified above and how you can encourage and advance them and their success.

See what you notice by focusing more on others and their success. It will be a rewarding break from yourself!

DEVELOP THE CAPACITY OF OTHERS

When you are a leader, your highest calling is to develop the capacity of others—to leave people more capable and empowered because of your relationship with them. Let's call those people *The Talent*. We do this by directing, advising, teaching, mentoring, and coaching the people in our lives.

The first step is to pay more attention to what others are doing and saying than we might normally. Does it seem like they're not on the right track? Or perhaps they're just a hair away from where they need to be. Then, if the situation allows (there are times when you'll have no option other than to step in), ask them what they're thinking, what they need, or if they even want help.

Different circumstances call for different types of support. Here's how to recognize when each approach is most helpful:

DIRECTING

In some cases, people need to be told exactly what to do, especially in situations that are new, complex, or high-risk.

A new employee is about to run their first high-stakes client meeting. You might say, "Here's the structure I want you to follow. Start with introductions, clarify the client's objectives, then walk them through our three-point proposal. I'll sit in and debrief with you afterward."

This is *directing*—providing clarity, expectations, and specific steps when someone simply doesn't have the experience yet. Or in an emergency situation, it sounds like "You, go call 911. Now."

ADVISING

When someone is more experienced but facing a decision where your insights could add value, you offer *advice* rather than direction.

A direct report is choosing between two vendors. You might say, "In my experience, Vendor A is more flexible, but Vendor B has always delivered on time. Given your deadline, that might matter more here."

You're not making the decision for them, but you're offering an informed perspective to guide their thinking.

TEACHING

Sometimes, people need to be taught a new skill or provided with information they don't yet possess.

A teammate is struggling to give effective presentations. You might say, "Let me show you how to build a strong argument that supports your message. Start with the key idea, then structure your points with supporting data and visuals. Then, you need to end with one clear ask."

Teaching is about *imparting knowledge*—helping others build competence and confidence.

MENTORING

Mentoring goes deeper. It's about long-term development, expanding someone's network, and offering access and opportunity.

A high-potential team member expresses a desire to transition into leadership. You might respond, "Let's get you exposure to more strategic meetings. I'll also connect you with someone who made a similar transition and can share what helped them."

Mentors provide guidance, connections, and belief in someone's long-term growth.

COACHING

Above all, and as you know at this point, outstanding leaders coach. This means helping others access their own best thinking, creativity, and capability.

A colleague tells you they're overwhelmed with their team's performance. Rather than offer immediate solutions, you ask, "What do you think is contributing to the current dynamic? What do you think you want to do next?"

You help them clarify their thinking, uncover insights, and take ownership of their path forward.

COACHING IMPACT
Developing the capacity of others

Tell

Ask

The Talent

IMPACT

Leader Coach

| Directing | Advising | Teaching | Mentoring | Coaching |

INNERLIFE LEADERSHIP
SUSANNE BIRO INC.

In short, you want to accomplish the following:

- **Direct (Tell):** Communicate the vision, values, mission, culture, roles, and responsibilities clearly and effectively.
- **Advise:** Offer insight that supports key decisions and responsibilities.
- **Teach:** Impart knowledge, skills, and greater self-awareness.
- **Mentor:** Provide guidance, visibility, connections, and growth opportunities.
- **Coach (Ask):** Help others access and act on their own best thinking and potential.

The most effective leaders know how to skillfully shift between these roles, adapting to the person and the moment. The real art is knowing when to direct, when to advise, when to teach, when to mentor, and when to ask, listen, and coach.

No matter what the situation, your aim is always the same: leave people stronger and more capable because of how you showed up. Whenever possible, start with coaching.

APPLY THE IDEA: LEAD WITH INTENTION

Direct. Advise. Teach. Mentor. Coach.

Write these five words on a sticky note and keep it near your computer.

Before meetings, ask yourself: *What is most needed from me with this person or audience?*

Then, discipline yourself to *ask rather than tell* whenever possible.

The goal is not to have all the answers. It's to teach others how to think for themselves and trust their own highest counsel.

THE FOUR KEY COACHING TOOLS: ACKNOWLEDGMENT, QUESTIONS, INTUITION, AND SILENCE

There are four foundational tools all great executive coaches use to support exceptional performance in others: Acknowledgment, Questions, Intuition, and Silence.

Watch any masterful communicator—an inspiring leader, trusted advisor, gifted interviewer, beloved teacher, or thoughtful parent—and you'll likely see these tools in action.

Acknowledgment: *"I see you. I see who you are and who you are working to become."*

Great coaches are first-class observers. They see the potential of others clearly, and they voice what they see. They also notice when someone is falling short and are willing to get curious and have the necessary conversation.

Acknowledgment is not flattery. It communicates: *You matter. I'm paying attention.*

Questions: *"How are you? What do you most want? What do you need?"*

Great leaders ask real questions. They ask open-ended questions because they are genuinely curious to learn and know more versus asking leading questions that are really just judgments and advice masked as questions. Real questions invite deep reflection, spark insight, and ignite ownership. One well-timed question can unlock someone's clarity and motivation more powerfully than a dozen directives.

In a blog post titled 30 Great Coaching Questions on www.SusanneBiro.com, I provide a list of questions you can use to foster excitement, engagement, motivation, and clarity in others. Use them to help others choose their best path as they navigate the challenges and opportunities that come their way.

Intuition: *"I'm noticing something..."*

As we progress through our lives and careers, we gain deep insight and experience—wisdom that becomes a powerful source of intuitive knowing. We *see* things in others, situations, and the choices they make. We pick up patterns. We get gut-level red flags. This is an extraordinary gift, but too often we dismiss or suppress it (which is why we started this book with the importance of self-trust).

As a coach, your intuition is vital. You don't want to sit silently while someone retells the same story that keeps them stuck in a limitation or a state of victimhood. Nor do you want to just ask questions while someone flounders, unaware they are missing critical information. You have too much perspective, care, and experience to hold back.

But how you share your insight matters. Note how the following examples offer your intuition as your perspective, not as the truth.

- "It seems to me..."
- "I'm wondering if..."

- "I might be off here, but I'm noticing…"
- "Here's what I am thinking… "

Follow up with an open-ended question for deeper discussion.

- "Does that hold any truth for you?"
- "What part resonates or doesn't?"
- "If that were true, how would it shift your thinking or actions?"

When you do this, you're not pushing your opinion; you're offering a deeper lens and inviting the other person to consider it, expand it, or discard it. When you do this genuinely, with care and curiosity, others can hear and will consider your perspective.

And remember: The more self-aware you are, the more trust you'll have in your own insight, and you'll be able to naturally use it in the service of others to have the *one conversation*.

To deepen your ability to do this, integrate these key tools throughout your leadership and coaching practice:

- **Self-Inquiry Tool (SIT)** (See chapter four)
  Use this tool to surface and examine the emotions, fears, patterns, and stories at play inside of you so you don't project them onto others, and so you can lead calmly and with clarity.
- **One Conversation. Walk Away Empty.** (See chapter six)
  Learn to say what's essential—so you don't walk away holding back what might have made a difference.

- **Real Conversations: The Five Questions Worksheet**
  (See chapter six)

  Build on the SIT by preparing yourself to have the real conversation playing out now in the confines of your own heart and mind.

These tools help you gain a deeper understanding of yourself, access the insights you already possess, and trust your voice more often, so you can show up as the leader and coach others need.

Silence: *Bite your tongue. Listen deeply.*

Silence is one of the most underused leadership tools. When used effectively, it invites others to tap into their own clarity and wisdom. It also shows that you are listening, not just waiting to speak.

The more you use silence, the more powerful your conversations become. Few people actually do this well, so if you learn to master your ability to listen and be present, you will be rare and impactful.

Try this:

Take some time and practice using these four tools in your next interaction.

- Pay close attention to someone today. Acknowledge what you see in their effort or circumstances.
- Ask an open-ended question.
- Offer a thoughtful reflection from your intuition, your perspective. Be brave. Don't hold back.

- Be quiet. Give them space to think, speak, and find their own clarity.

See what shifts when you lead this way. The real power of leadership is not in knowing more—it's in helping others know themselves better.

APPLY THE IDEA: REAL CONVERSATIONS

As I pointed out in chapter six, conversations are not just important to leadership; they *are* leadership.

Grab the Five Questions Worksheet and think of someone you sincerely care about and want to succeed (this could be your child, spouse, a direct report, a good friend, or even your boss). Complete the worksheet to gain clarity on what you are genuinely thinking and what you honestly want. Your answers to these five questions will often be the exact conversation you want and need to have. Your answers are your script or talking points, which you might even share exactly as you write them out.

COACHING AND DEVELOPING OTHERS: GENEROSITY

Coaching is an act of generosity.

To be an outstanding coach, you must step outside your comfort zone and take risks solely to benefit the person you're developing. You may need to take risks like asking difficult questions or fully acknowledging another when their talent and success threaten your own sense of self-worth.

Coaching is the act of providing another human being with everything you would love to have: attention, kindness, compassion, truth, and love—*fierce love!* It's about enabling them to be seen, not merely for what they are today but also for all they still dream of becoming tomorrow. Few can demonstrate this level of selflessness and generosity. However, those who do can have an immense impact.

It also requires you to listen fully, without interrupting or speaking just to feel seen or validated. In its simplest form, this is an act of generosity: making a conversation or relationship valuable for the other person without needing anything in return. Few of us do this regularly, because it asks us to set aside our own needs, even if just momentarily. But if you're unsure how often you do it, try this: In your next conversation, focus entirely on the other person. Resist the urge to redirect the topic or insert your own experience. Just listen to make that moment meaningful for them alone.

To be an effective coach, you need to focus on the needs and success of someone else solely to benefit them. To fully help others, you must first undertake the challenging inner work of recognizing and overcoming the negative mindset that hinders your own growth and success, thereby positioning yourself to assist others effectively. The most outstanding leaders are those who have done the inner work to understand their own patterns, beliefs, and blind spots—because it is from that awareness that compassion, clarity, and presence emerge.

That is the entire purpose of this book: to help you do your own inner work so you can live well, lead well, and ultimately serve and advance our world as only you can. You are more impactful and influential than you know.

Everything you've read until now has led to this chapter. This is the moment where your inner growth becomes outer impact.

So take these tools into your conversations, your conflicts, and your quietest moments. Practice them not as techniques but as a way of being. You'll find that the more you help others rise, the higher you go. And that is the true power and privilege of leadership.

CHAPTER NINE

LEADERSHIP FOR A NEW WORLD

Now that we've come this far, I hope you realize that being a leader has little to do with holding a leadership title, having a team, or even having followers.

However, it does have everything to do with knowing yourself, hearing and validating your thoughts and feelings, and then having the courage to act upon your own highest, inner knowing.

Whether you are the seasoned CEO of a multibillion-dollar enterprise, a first-time manager, or a stay-at-home parent raising the next generation, the essence of true leadership is the same—trust thy (highest) self.

As you now understand well, becoming ourselves takes awareness, effort, and work, and it is necessary for living an enjoyable, meaningful life. This means that unfortunately (but ultimately, *fortunately*), there's absolutely no way you can escape doing it.

You see, it won't matter what path you take in life because, rest assured, life will bring you the exact people and circumstances to force you to stop, look within, and examine yourself. You must face yourself: your fears, insecurities, and pain. Leadership amplifies how greatly you must first reckon with yourself before you can begin to serve others.

The only choice is whether you will work with what you find inside.

You will either choose to become more—more self-aware, open, loving, curious, humble, and gracious—or you will gradually become less—a smaller, more limited, negative, judgmental, and bitter version of yourself.

Everyone has this choice available to them. But not everyone decides to do their (inner) work.

Some double down on their old ways of thinking and feeling and become ever more desperate, dysfunctional, and disconnected. Filled with negativity, criticism, fear, judgments, and hatred, they create isolation, chaos, and divisiveness everywhere they go. They blame people and circumstances for their lot in life. They never grow up because they are unwilling to accept responsibility for taking the hand they were dealt and playing the hell out of it. This is the antithesis of leadership.

Others stay distracted and fail to decide who they will be, and then they also become a lesser version of who they actually are and who they most wanted and hoped to be in life! They wonder where all the time has gone and feel like they've missed the starting line.

As we close out this book, I want to leave you with a few final reflections. These are truths for you to carry with you as you decide who you will be and how you will lead from here.

WHAT WILL YOU DO WITH THE HAND YOU'RE DEALT?

One of the first truths we must confront is this: We don't all begin from the same place. The hand we're dealt—our circumstances, upbringing, and access to resources—helps determine what our choices look like.

Yes, some started with an amazing set of cards to play. And some were given a heartbreaking deck. If this is you, I'm so sorry. But what is most telling is that you are here reading this book. History is marked by those, like you, who took the hand they were dealt and made all they could with it for the time in which they lived.

They lived their lives.

They chased their dreams!

They stood for something timeless and important: peace, equality, justice, love, often in the face of torture and even death.

These leaders died with inner pride, and it was enough. In fact, it was everything.

I am aware I was dealt a great hand: I had two parents who loved me, who wanted me, and who kept me safe. I only realized recently how rare it was that I was kept safe, when almost every other woman I know was not. I was born in Canada. I am Caucasian. I've never had to go without water, food, or a roof over my head. And on top of all these blessings, I had access to an education and the opportunity for steady, decent work, so I alone could pay for it. I was born into privilege and power.

We might all be running the same course, but without a doubt, we start at very different places and have very different opportunities available to us.

Power and privilege matter. Greatly. However, this short book does not address the vast implications of power and privilege. Allan G. Johnson's *Privilege, Power, and Difference* is a brilliant exploration of this topic. I strongly recommend reading it.

In my book, I have hoped only to (re)connect you with yourself so you can become your highest self and enjoy the inner pride that comes when you see yourself as a person and leader worthy of your own respect.

There is something priceless about looking in the mirror when no one else is around and seeing someone who chose to do what was good and right over what was lazy, self-serving, or deceitful. The alternative is a quiet torment—the lingering ache of regret and the sharp sting of missed opportunities. It is the realization that things could have been so different if only we had been more open, more at ease with ourselves and others, less rigid in our thinking, and less ruled by feelings we never learned to handle. When we betray our own integrity, we can never fully escape the shadow of our own shame. It follows us into the quiet moments, reminding us that the hardest person to live with is the one we see in the mirror.

True leaders embrace their humanity, take full responsibility for their lives, and in doing so, become a light for others.

Because you've read this book to the end, I suspect this is you.

TO BE HUMAN IS TO STRUGGLE

Of course, you won't achieve your goals without inner struggle and deep self-reflection.

Being human is hard, and striving to be a good and successful one who is truly in touch with yourself is even harder. But it's not as hard as the alternative: never really knowing yourself, reacting unconsciously with the same habitual thoughts, or never questioning your own motivations. That path leads only to a personal hell I wouldn't wish on my worst enemy. The only real choice is growth, because growth is freedom. Everything else is bondage.

In his book, *The Road Less Traveled*, author M. Scott Peck makes the claim that life is difficult. On the surface, I agree. Being a spiritual entity in a heavy, physical body on this dark, dense, material plane is definitely no picnic. Our bodies never look how we want them to look, they rarely function as we hope, they break down often, and, eventually, they fail each and every one of us. This is one thing we know for certain. Of course, life is difficult!

I know I am so much more than I can show you in this physical form and in the short amount of time I have in my human life. I suspect you feel the same. This is why many of us cannot accept the present moment. It is also why so many of us focus our time and energy solely on getting to what we believe will be a better place, whether that is the next moment or an afterlife.

Far too many of us spend our entire lives trying to "make it" in this world, competing so we can finally enjoy our lives. What we rarely realize is the reason we never "arrive" or "win" is that there is no place to get to and there never was a competition. Yet, we spend our very short lives living as if there was—and then we die.

Is that funny? Painfully so.

Life does not need to be as challenging and painful as many of us experience it to be daily. A great deal of our suffering can be self-inflicted. I don't doubt that something may have happened to you that was wrong (sometimes terribly wrong), but what I want you to realize is that you are now continuing the pain by the thoughts you think, the identity you have formed around key life events, and the story you rehearse to yourself daily, and then feel compelled to act out over and over and *over* again.

The story you are telling yourself isn't true; it is merely one story. As we have progressed through this book, please be aware now that there are others. This idea is powerfully illustrated in *The Death of Ivan Ilyich* by Leo Tolstoy, when the main character asks on his deathbed, "What if my whole life has been wrong?"[22] His question reveals the kind of painful clarity that often arrives too late, reminding us to examine our choices now, before we reach the end and realize we could have lived so differently if we only decided to.

---

22   Tolstoy, Leo. *The Death of Ivan Ilyich*. Translated by Louise and Aylmer Maude. New York: Bantam Classics, 1981.

By sharing this, I hope I have offered you hope, an awakening, and an entirely new way to experience life and yourself in it. But as you well know by now, this new life won't come from working harder. It will come only from surrendering, from a *complete change of mind.*

The beginning of peace and freedom is to be yourself, fully and completely, in each moment. At any time, you can simply choose to be present to the person or task right in front of you. It is the possibility of a life not bound by the constraints of having to maintain an identity. It is the possibility of freedom, a life filled with *presence.*

Please consider this: You are *exactly* where you need to be. Relax. Don't judge what has occurred or what is occurring as good or bad. Just be. Focus yourself to be fully present for the next person or task that you face. Bring your whole self and full attention to the moment. Repeat as often as you remember throughout your day. See what you notice.

THE SAME THOUGHTS WON'T CREATE A NEW FUTURE

Many of our daily thoughts are repetitive in nature—replaying worries, predicting future scenarios, or rehashing past events. This mental loop may help explain why, even after major changes, successes, or achievements, our lives feel the same because we are mentally stuck in the same patterns.

Interestingly, have you ever noticed how much of your internal dialogue is focused on yourself—your desires, needs, and aspirations? Often, we don't realize just how habitual and self-absorbed our thought patterns have become.

Reflecting on this, one of my favorite quotes, attributed to Wei Wu Wei is "Why are you unhappy? Because 99.99% of everything you think about and all that you do is for yourself—and there isn't one."[23] This speaks to the irony of our condition: Most of us wander through life engrossed in our thoughts, focusing on our to-do lists, desires, and particularly, on how others perceive us, striving to influence their perceptions to match our desires.

This preoccupation may seem comical, yet tragically, it consumes most of us, which Buddhists liken to sleepwalking through life.

Awakening, in this context, means becoming more present, being able to observe our immediate reality without dragging our personal histories into every present moment, and unknowingly creating the same life experience everywhere we go!

It's as if we've spent our lives wearing a virtual reality headset, where we are engrossed in the narratives displayed on our personal screens, rarely interacting with the world as it truly is but rather as we expect it to be. When faced with real-life situations, like a colleague rushing into our office upset, our initial interpretations are filtered through our personal biases and emotions, demonstrating our tendency to project our reality onto the situation, rather than seeing it for what it truly is.

Our immediate assumptions may vary widely—from fearing their emotional state is directed at us, believing we've done

---

23   Wei Wu Wei. Open Secret. Hong Kong: Hong Kong University Press, 1964.

something wrong, to interpreting their behavior as a sign of trust and seeing ourselves as a confidant. Sometimes, we may sigh, thinking, *I always attract the emotional ones*, or wonder, *Why must I always shoulder others' burdens?* But by consciously acknowledging what we are witnessing—simply stating, "You seem hurried and upset," we begin to engage authentically.

Follow this acknowledgment with clear communication of our boundaries. This can be "I don't have time to talk today, but let's schedule a time tomorrow," or "I can spare five minutes now; what do you need most?" Or invite them in with "Shut my door, let's talk." By speaking and acting in this way, we not only honor our own limited capacity but also the other person's immediate needs. This fosters a deeper connection and understanding. When we learn to notice our self-orienting, repetitive thinking, we can begin to shift our focus and think anew. How exciting!

ARE YOU A HORSE OR A DOG?

One key concept I teach to my clients is the "horse and dog analogy." It's a perspective I've found universally applicable across professions. Here it is: I have often thought that if I were an animal, I would be a horse, as I am extremely sensitive. As you may know, a horse is a prey animal (versus a predator), and thus it is constantly scanning its environment for safety, often mirroring the emotions of others, not unlike many humans. Years ago, I found myself often adapting my behavior based on others' reactions—diminishing my enthusiasm around those who were distant or rushing to match the pace of those who appeared anxious. The result was that I was never very comfortable in the presence of others. How could I have been?

I was always watching what others did and then trying to adapt myself.

But when I have observed the successful professionals I admire, I notice their consistent, friendly, and approachable demeanor, which has led me to reevaluate my approach. Instead of mirroring emotions like a horse, I considered what a dog does. A dog is always welcoming, regardless of the recipient's mood. The dog always sets a positive tone for every interaction.

As a dog, I would no longer match emotion for emotion. Instead, I would set the tone for all my relationships. I would ensure that my actions stemmed from my friendly yet honest personable state, regardless of how others acted or reacted. Rather than scanning for safety and mirroring other people, I would make it safe and take their behaviors as important information for me to understand, share, and then coach or challenge them on. This shift from reacting to leading in relationships promised a more constructive engagement with others, especially in challenging professional scenarios.

This analogy was particularly notable during a session with a senior leader at a biotech company in San Francisco, California. The day of our meeting, I waited a while for this busy executive to arrive in the designated office. When he finally showed up 15 minutes late, he started by saying, "Look, I don't know how much my company is paying you, but you have 45 minutes, and this better be good."

Rather than reacting in a hostile manner to match his, I stood up, smiled, and said, "Good morning! My name is Susanne Biro. It is great to meet you. Now that's a very interesting way to introduce yourself to someone. Please sit down; let's talk about it." So we did.

I asked him if his "prove-yourself-to-me" approach worked well for him. He shared he only showed up that way with some people but not with others. We discussed when this was effective and, by his own assessment, when it was not. We also talked about other approaches and what had occurred for him earlier in the day that contributed to his brash demeanor. Then we explored how he might better manage himself for ultimate effectiveness.

The next day, I received an email in which he thanked me for my insight into his behavior and shared how few had ever called him out on it. He said he "got it" and would be making some adjustments.

Too often we react to others' ineffective ways of being in the world. Someone is short or rude with us, and before we know it, we are triggered and then only able to return the same. There is a better way, however. If we are leaders, then we must master our own reactions, and like a friendly dog, set the tone for our relationships.

Being a caring, self-aware, available, clear, direct, and gracious mentor, teacher, and coach to others is the real work of leadership. Of course, this takes maturity, patience, work, and nothing short of our own personal development.

Each of us will either do our own work and excel, or we will soon find ourselves irrelevant to the humanity our world needs and wants now.

THE POWER OF PRESENCE

Some of the world's best leaders have been called charismatic. This is true. The best, most successful men and women I have ever met or worked with have all had the ability to be present. In fact, some are so present with us that time ceases to exist. The force of their personality creates a feeling of space and timelessness. In their presence, we feel like the most important person in the room.

I learned the true power of presence the first time I met Sir Richard Branson. He's a role model to millions, and after growing up seeing him on TV, he was, and still is, a celebrity to me.

In 2016, I was invited to an entrepreneurs' event on his private island. Coming from a blue-collar household, I thought it might be a scam. I thought *Why me?* I later discovered several other guests felt the same way!

On the first night on Necker Island, about 30 of us were gathered around the bar in his main house. We were chatting casually when in walked Richard. Saying I was starstruck would be an understatement. Yet, he approached each of us, introduced himself warmly, and connected personally. When he approached me, he said how much he loved Canada and asked about the wildfires that my home province had been battling at the time. He was genuinely interested. He was fully present.

Later that week, I sat across from him at dinner. I watched as he gave his full attention to the person on his left, right, and then to me. I asked him questions I was eager to ask, and he answered thoughtfully and graciously. He continued that rhythm, turning toward each guest with care and interest. I've met several personal heroes in my life, but Richard was the only one to live up to all the praise.

I believe great people are generous in this way. They give their full attention to whatever and whoever is in front of them. Mastery is treating each interaction not as a means to something else but as an end in itself.

Presence is being all there. It means not checking our phones but truly engaging with people. As Simon Sinek says, even holding your phone sends the message that someone else is second to your device. We should treat people as Maya Angelou said parents should treat children: "Your eyes should light up when your child enters the room."[24] Adults need this too. It's why we love dogs. They see us—really see us.

So how do we become more present?

We start by putting our phones away. That's advice I need to follow myself, but it's important. Let others see you do it. It tells them they matter to you.

When someone enters the room, look at them and stand up. Signal to yourself that a new moment has begun. Acknowledge them.

Before client sessions, I clear my desk of anything I had been working on to signal that the next hour is all about them. I then review my notes and center myself to be present to who comes

---

24 Maya Angelou, interview by Bill Moyers, The Power of Words, Bill Moyers Journal, PBS, 1988.

to my call—not who I spoke to at the last session, as their lives can change greatly in between sessions.

No matter what personal or professional challenges I may be facing, clearing my desk helps me close down my life so I can be fully present for someone else. I often remind myself: "These problems will wait for me." And they always do!

This simple act has become a kind of gift. Focusing on others is often a welcome break from myself. It reminds me that very little is about me. Immersing oneself in someone else's world can bring us clarity and a fresh perspective. As Albert Schweitzer said, "The only ones among you who will be really happy are those who will have sought and found how to serve."

Here's how to practice this today:

- Put your phone away, and let others see you do it.
- Look people in the eyes. See their faces. Whether on Zoom or in person—or even just hearing their voice on the phone—*be all there.*
- Before meetings, clear your desk or change your space. Your work will wait. Turn your attention fully to the people and the task at hand.
- Use the act of walking through a doorway as a mental cue to become present.
- Spend time with someone you experience as exceptionally present. Learn from them. Being on the receiving end is so rewarding and enjoyable, it will encourage and inspire you to be the same with others.

- Revisit your Daily Disciplines (in chapter 5) and do the things that enable you to be most available for others because you first took care of your needs.

It has been said that we all want to be loved the way no one can love, but what if you could? Your presence is more powerful than you know.

A TSUNAMI OF CHANGE

Even as we learn to anchor ourselves in presence, the world around us is undergoing radical, accelerating change, demanding that we enter this entirely new terrain.

Several years ago, I completed the Singularity Executive Program, deeply exploring exponential technologies that are set to transform how we live and work. Since then, I've stayed connected with countless thought leaders at the forefront of technology and artificial intelligence. Their insights make one thing clear: The pace of change is accelerating faster than anyone predicted.

In a world reshaped so rapidly and unpredictably, the one thing we can control is how we respond. The most vital skills for this new era are deeply human: adaptability, empathy, and compassion.

We must learn to be on our own side, offering ourselves grace, compassion, and encouragement. An inner life filled with harsh self-criticism will not sustain us. Technology will soon surpass human intelligence, and we do not yet know the very real implications to our work and our lives. To survive and, more so, thrive, we must learn to love our human journey. It is so beautiful how much we care about what others think of us and how much we each want to both help and impress others. It might be my favorite thing about humans. What is your favorite thing about people?

HUMOR AND HUMANITY!

The best advice I ever got was to "Chill the fuck out!" The advice came from my sister, who I already shared is the kindest and most loving human being you might ever meet. She rarely swears, so when she said this, she got my attention, broke my thought process, and made me laugh.

Humor and our own humanity might be some of the most underrated skills in leadership, again, defined as working exceptionally well with and through others. My sister went on to add, "You are so tightly wound, you are driving the rest of us crazy!"

Like many of my clients, I'm definitely Type A. To me, that reflects my desire to succeed. I decided that early in life, and for years, I drove myself with thoughts that I needed to do more, have more, become somebody who is more. My rehearsed quality of mind was: "You are not enough right now, but when you get this, achieve that, have those things, get invited there, etc., you will finally arrive, and then you can be yourself, relax, and enjoy your life!" Sound familiar?

For years, I didn't realize I was lost in a thought pattern of "When I get X, then I will have Y."

My sister's advice and humor broke my pattern and brought me to the present, so I could experience what I was really seeking: the ability to enjoy life!

If you have ever tried to align a group of people, you know how frustrating it can be. Everyone comes with their own vision, values, ideas, motivations, life circumstances, unique personalities, cultures, languages, and ways of communicating. Whether you are deciding which movie to watch with your family (ours can take over an hour to decide, at which point we no longer feel like watching a movie together!) or leading an organization through a significant change, aligning human beings is hard, often frustrating work.

So having a sense of humor, bringing some appropriate levity into it all, can make all the difference.

We really do need to remember that the sole purpose of leadership is to make life better in some meaningful way. As I said earlier in this book, let's not make our own and other people's lives a living hell while we attempt to do so.

If we are to improve the world, we must improve the world of the people we interact with today, while working together to make tomorrow better for us all.

The best leaders I have ever worked with all had a wonderful knack for making light of serious work. This took the edge off, making the stress of the work and deadlines enjoyable and exciting, as we felt united and supported.

My first career was as an advertising executive. With typical determination, I constantly drove myself to succeed. One

Friday afternoon, the agency CEO walked by my desk and said to me, "If you don't stop working and start drinking with us, we will fire you!" She was kidding, of course. But it reminded me that connecting with my colleagues mattered and that I needed to know when to stop driving myself and others hard.

The best leaders know that humor connects us and that being able to laugh at ourselves is a superpower.

The truth is that life works because a lot of people do things we can't or don't want to do. I have no idea how electricity works, but I'm wildly grateful every time the lights come on. The same is true for planes, plumbing, and algorithms. Thank you, other humans.

That's why the best leaders know how to stay in their lane, do their part well, and deeply appreciate others who carry the rest. It's also why humor matters. It reminds us we're not alone in our limitations or ridiculousness.

Comedians show us this every time they make us laugh at the exact thing we were upset about yesterday. A dumb argument with your partner? Suddenly, we find it hilarious when someone else replays it with levity. We laugh because it's all so human.

Yes, take the work seriously. Build the thing. Lead the team. Just don't forget to find a way to laugh when your plan implodes, your technology fails, or your teenager gives you an attitude at home. Life is absurd. Leadership is too. Bring appropriate levity and laughter to the chaos, and you might just become someone others want to follow and actually enjoy the ride yourself.

YOUR NOW "NEXT LEVEL"

As a senior leadership coach, I am a human behaviorist, an avid reader, and a lifelong student. I know that working on myself is a nonnegotiable requirement for effectively helping others. I wish I could tell you this inner work has always come easily, that I've been a willing and eager student of my own development, but that would be a lie.

In my masters program, I remember telling my professors, who had gently encouraged me to see the on-staff counselor, that while some of my classmates might need that kind of help, I certainly did not. I'm sure they struggled to keep a straight face. The irony isn't lost on me. I was pursuing a master's degree to help leaders better understand themselves, their impact, and their interactions with others; yet, I wasn't willing to do the same. Worse still, I actually believed I didn't have any personal work to do. Isn't that some kind of arrogance?

Even now, I struggle to master myself, my thoughts, my reactions (especially with my husband), and my commitment to caring for my physical body. I eat primarily foods with only one ingredient, and I practice yoga, yet I can still fall into old patterns, whether it's consuming too much sugar or the recurring illusion that I need to become "someone" or get "somewhere" to finally be okay. I've often whispered, "When do I get to arrive?"

I see this, too, in my clients. The belief that "X must happen so Y can" is deeply ingrained. But that thinking doesn't lead to happiness—or even to true accomplishment. If you've recognized this pattern in yourself, take heart. That realization is not small. It's a vital milestone on the path to deep fulfillment.

After thousands of conversations with senior leaders, I've learned this: The answers to our outer challenges are found only through inner solutions. You can focus on shaping your outer life, and perhaps your inner life will follow. But when you focus on your inner life, your outer life transforms.

I could be endlessly frustrated that life doesn't match my expectations. Or I can embrace reality for what it offers: the opportunity to learn, grow, and become more! I know I've barely scratched the surface of my own development. Oddly enough, that excites me.

It's liberating to admit that I don't know exactly what should occur or what will make me truly happy. I can stop trying to control the world to bring me the perfect circumstances, something it has never done, anyway. Instead, I can show up for what *is occurring*. I can ask, "What is needed now? With this person? In this moment?" When I follow life's lead, I always know what to do. And I often yield much better results because I'm no longer fixated on what *should* be happening. As a result, I can deal with what *is*.

Is that what freedom is? I believe so.

The only place we ever truly live is inside ourselves.

If you seek success, fulfillment, and joy in the uncertain years ahead, your work will be an inside job. The best part? You need nothing outside of you to change—not your job, not your family, not your body. Everything that happens is an opportunity to practice being good in this moment, right now.

Love is the most powerful force on the planet. It is the answer to any question we might ask, and it begins with the love we extend to ourselves as we navigate this messy, painful, beautiful human life. Even when, perhaps especially when, we sit in horror at world events, our inner state matters.

What we cultivate within, we will experience and create around us. Peace begins within. The true purpose of life is to become okay inside. Start there now.

This could be everything, if you let it.

The life ahead of you will be shaped by the thoughts and feelings you nurture within, so choose them with care. Decide who you will be, and train your mind to speak to you with kindness, encouragement, and fierce love—the kind of love that the best mom or dad you can imagine would give you. Do this on your good days, on your bad days, and most especially, on your darkest days. You have never been this age, dealing with all you are dealing with, and if you are here reading this book, then you are doing so well.

This human journey is hard, yet you are walking it, and you are needed more than you know. You have the power to make someone's day. Your light, your kindness, and your courage matter, and they will ripple out and impact those you will never meet. You have the power to lift others, to make the world more human, more compassionate, **and more alive with love!**

This is what it means to lead.

And it begins here, by finally choosing to love yourself in all your imperfect, beautiful, messy humanity. Love is not just an answer; it is the answer—the one you have been searching for your entire life.

You've arrived at the final page, and that is no small thing. It means you showed up, stayed with the journey, and invested in yourself, and that is worth celebrating! Please do something today to show yourself you're living what you've taken from this book.

And as I tell every client, I will always love to hear from you. Please share your story, insight, or win on LinkedIn or any social media platform. Connect and tag me @SusanneBiro. Let's celebrate together, because a win for any one of us is a win for us all.

Stay in touch with me at www.SusanneBiro.com by joining my inner circle and connecting with me on social media.

ABOUT THE AUTHOR

Susanne Biro is an executive coach with over two decades of international experience working with CEOs, executive-level leaders, and their teams at some of the world's most respected organizations. Her work focuses on elevating executive effectiveness, communication, and whole-life success.

www.ingramcontent.com/pod-product-compliance
Lightning Source LLC
Chambersburg PA
CBHW071200210326
41597CB00016B/1618